A
PICTURE HISTORY
OF THE
Automobile

by Peter Roberts

Ward Lock Ltd, London

Acknowledgments

'Autocar' 37b, 38b, 40t
Conway Library 59
Mary Evans 5 (both), 9b
Imperial War Museum 95, 97r, 97b, 97t
Louis Klementaski 118, 119
Mansell Collection 7, 34t
'Motor Cycle' 38t
National Motor Museum 69b, 69r, 71b, 72b,
    110t, 110b, 111, 112b, 114 (both)
National Portrait Gallery 6t
Radio Times Hulton Library 6b, 37t, 45t,
    45l, 71t, 98b, 119
Peter Roberts 24, 25, 28, 29 (all), 32, 52, 53,
    56b, 66l, 75b, 81, 92 (all), 93 (all), 124, 125
Science Museum 8, 9t
Veteran Car Club of Great Britain 68, 70t

*The author and publishers also offer their thanks to
the following manufacturers for their help in
supplying photographs (often very rare) and
information: Citroën, Renault, Peugeot, Simca,
Opel, Daimler-Benz, Porsche, Volkswagen, Audi
NSU, Fiat, Ferrari, Alfa Romeo, Lancia, Pirelli,
Datsun, Rover, BLMC, Chrysler UK and
International General Motors, Ford Great Britain
and USA, and Horsfall & Bickham*

ISBN 0 7063 1301 1
First published in 1973 by
Ward Lock Ltd, London, England
Revised edition 1974
© Trewin Copplestone Publishing Ltd, 1973
Printed in Great Britain by
Ben Johnson & Company Ltd.,
York, England.

Contents

Preface

Around ninety years ago, when Gottlieb Daimler and Karl Benz were building their first self-propelled petrol-driven road vehicles—at an identical moment in history, unknown to each other and not more than sixty miles apart in two small German towns—the age of the motor car became inevitable.

From those small, tentative experiments in Mannheim and Canstatt – Benz making his spindly three-wheeler and Daimler his clanking converted coach—the world's motor scene grew. So did the new and wonderful personal freedom the car brought with it, a mobility that was as important to the social revolution of the first half of the twentieth century as that other great catalyst of change, radio communication.

The single-cylinder, one-horse-power carriages developed with astonishing rapidity over the ensuing twenty years, becoming powerful vehicles, with a layout (thanks greatly to the experiments of French designer and builder Emile Levassor) roughly the same as most conventional cars today. During those years, the commercial manufacture of automobiles spread to most of the industrial countries of the world. Towns that had been linked by rail or plodding horse became more casually accessible to each other and people began to meet each other more regularly and often than ever before in history. It should have led to something fine; our grandfathers certainly thought it would, and put money and a great deal of innocent faith into the motor car, the transport that would lead to a new confraternity of mankind. . .

Early motor sport—as inevitable as motoring itself—accelerated the development of the automobile, until in the great Paris–Vienna race of 1902, 70 hp and 70 mph were already not unusual.

Most of the tenets of automobile engineering were laid down during the first fifteen years of the automobile's existence, and most of them were adhered to for half a century. The years that followed were mainly years of improvement and development, when the work of the pioneers was refined rather than rendered obsolete.

In this book we look at the story of motoring in a survey of the pattern of developments that led up to the automobile of today. The foundations of the industry—in some ways also the foundations of our present economy, heavily influenced as it is by the automobile—are seen in the chapters on the first two 'fathers of the automobile', Benz and Daimler. The early story of four of the men whose foresight and energy laid the cornerstones of four great companies is outlined and some of the exploits of early racing drivers are illustrated.

So into the brash 'twenties, great days for the great marques. Rolls-Royce was already a synonym for perfection. Bentley, Hispano-Suiza and Isotta Fraschini, the marques beloved of the novelist. Ettore Bugatti, who had been making exquisite cars since 1909, produced in 1927 his famous sporting Type 43, while in the United States a year later, the truly astonishing Model J Duesenberg appeared. The economic pressures of the 'twenties encouraged the further development of small cheap cars, and during the 'thirties, in Europe at least, these swamped the market and the roads, and the period has become known for a rapid increase in the numbers of vehicles and its unfortunate corollary, a rapid decline in quality.

In Europe, if not in the United States, the 'thirties are the years no one wants to know, and from the design viewpoint the decade was, with few exceptions, a desert. Nevertheless, the years before World War 2 were the halcyon years when millions tasted the heady exhilaration of mobility for the first time. Then for six grim years, motor manufacturers churned out war vehicles of various vicious designs, leaving us with the Jeep as our inheritance.

Immediately after the war, the world's car-makers cleaned up their mothballed tools—and began producing 1939 models once again. For several years, the public were so glad to get within touching distance of anything on wheels that they bought them up on sight, often having to contract to keep them for a couple of years before selling and making a handsome profit in a car-hungry market. The 'fifties with perhaps the Jaguar as the most distinguished car, have a chapter, and so has a subject at which even the boldest technical soothsayer writers often baulk: the probable classics of the future. A motoring 'calendar' pinpoints some of the historic highlights of the past, the modern Porsche factory is visited, and picture-spreads show the progress of several marques, from Ford to Rolls-Royce.

With fire and water

Some regard Karl Benz as the father of motoring, for he was the first to build cars for sale to the public. Others give the credit to Gottlieb Daimler, for his engines were the forerunners of all that followed.

Yet several people had built mechanically-propelled road vehicles before either of them, pioneers who came close to having their names venerated as those of Benz and Daimler are venerated, but who failed for one reason or another to consolidate their early success.

Some had the technical skill, but lacked the vision to see the new life-style that motoring would bring to the world. Some had the vision but lacked the practical ability to solve the problems that arose. Some had genius but lacked determination.

First of these forefathers of motoring, the men who might have been great, was a Frenchman, Nicholas Cugnot. He built the first mechanically-propelled vehicle in 1769.

Steam was his choice of power to replace the horse, and naturally so, for although this was still before the days of railways, stationary steam engines were in use for working winches and pumping water in mines.

Cugnot's invention was a steam tractor designed to tow guns for the French army. Basically it was a three-wheeled cart, on the floor of which was mounted a bench seat for the driver and three passengers. Over the leading wheel hung a huge copper cauldron. Steam raised by a coal fire entered two 50-litre cylinders and turned a large and heavy front wheel by rods.

The tractor worked – after a fashion. It lumbered along at two-and-a-bit miles an hour and ran out of steam every 10 minutes or so, but it impressed the army sufficiently to afford Cugnot the facilities of Louis XV's arsenal to develop it further.

The first self-propelled road vehicle – and the first motor accident: Cugnot and his steam tractor, 1769–70

Two years later Cugnot demonstrated an improved machine, hauling a four-ton gun, but the vehicle was appallingly ill-balanced and lacking in road holding. When the front wheel was turned to change direction the cauldron and engine turned with it, shifting the machine's centre of gravity. Inevitably the contraption overturned. The generals shook their heads and went back to their horses; Cugnot had created the first horseless vehicle, but he failed to sell it.

England's pioneers

Drawings of Cugnot's tractor reached England and were seen by William Murdock, assistant to James Watt, then the biggest name in steam power development. In 1784, Murdock set out to make his own steam vehicle, but modestly essayed only a scaled-down model. He used a spirit fire to create steam, and learning from Cugnot's mistakes, he mounted the engine over the rear wheels.

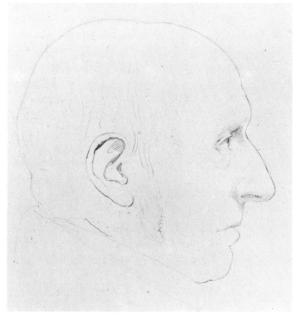

A contemporary sketch of Will Murdock

Britain's first steam vehicle, in a scaled-down model constructed by William Murdock, 1784

According to Cornish legend, Murdock road-tested his model one evening on a lane leading to the church in Redruth, where he lived. The vicar, meeting the hissing toy in the gloom, took to his heels. Later Murdock allowed himself to be taken off the project by Watt. Possibly Watt was motivated by jealousy; certainly Murdock never went the next step – building a full-size vehicle.

That was done, however, by Richard Trevithick, a mining engineer at Camborne, four miles away. With a tall chimney stack and a footplate for the fireman, his vehicle looked more like a railway locomotive than a car – but then the railway locomotive was also in the future.

On Christmas Eve, 1801, Trevithick took a party of his workmates for a ride on it. Eight people jumped aboard, eager to be the first travellers on the new machine. Wrote one of Trevithick's friends about that first journey: . . . 'When we see'd that Captain Dick was agoing to turn on steam, we jumped up, as many as could, maybe seven or eight of us. Twas a stiffish hill, but she went off like a bird . . .' Trevithick drove his steam-coach half a mile up that hill 'faster than a man could walk'. This journey and several later ones, gave Trevithick the distinction of being Britain's first motorist. But his pioneer machine, like Cugnot's, was not destined for a long career. Trevithick left it overnight in a hotel stables during one of his early demonstration runs. Unfortunately he forgot to extinguish the fire. The water boiled away and this historic vehicle was burnt to a shell.

With a cousin, Andrew Vivian, Trevithick built an improved version on which steam could be raised more quickly and maintained longer. Its coachwork was supported on wheels 10 ft. in diameter so that passengers rode six feet above the ground. Trevithick and Vivian drove it along London's Oxford Street, bumping and lurching over the ruts and terrifying the horses.

Yet, despite this enterprising piece of sales promotion, Trevithick found no sponsors. He sold the engine to power a mill, switched his interest to railways and designed stationary engines for winching trucks along rails. He died in poverty.

After the Napoleonic Wars, Britain's commerce, both abroad and at home, developed rapidly. Long-distance travel became part of the daily life of many merchants. The existing highways were in many places no more than country lanes, and powerful demands to improve the roads were made to local authorities.

Two men, both engineers, contributed greatly

to the improvement of the roads of those days, and indeed to the later introduction of self-propelled vehicles. Their names were Telford and Macadam. During the 1820s their road-building work enabled coach companies to set up a large and complex network of routes throughout the country helping, in no small way, the commercial and industrial prosperity of the nation.

During this time several far-sighted engineers developed the self-propelled steam coach, and by the 1830s several steam-coach companies operated regular passenger-carrying routes.

One of the more notable coach operators of the day was Sir Goldsworth Gurney, whose 'steam diligences' could carry up to 21 people and travel at 14 miles an hour at a cost of 3d a mile in coal.

In London several lines were opened, conveying passengers from London's East End to the City, and from Moorgate to Paddington, whilst other routes were opened from London to Bath and Cheltenham to Gloucester, each with timetables that were at least as reliable (and probably more so) than those of some of today's public transport systems.

By the late 1830s steam coaches were established and successful. But the horse-drawn coach companies and the new railway organisations feared that their trade would suffer from the rising competition. Strong representations were made to Parliament by railway and horse-coach owners, and in 1865 an Act of Parliament gave the *coup de grâce* to steam transport.

This was the notorious 'Red Flag Act' of 1865, which enacted that: **Firstly at least three persons shall be employed to drive or conduct such a locomotive . . .** (this alone greatly reduced a steam-coach company's profit) **. . . Secondly that one of such persons, while any locomotive is in motion, shall precede such locomotive on foot by not less than 60 yards, and shall carry a red flag constantly displayed . . .** It sounded the death-knell for steam coaches, and its existence was the major factor in delaying the later development of Britain's infant motor industry.

Meanwhile, in France and America, steam pioneers continued to build self-propelled vehicles, and by the latter part of the nineteenth century had designed vehicles that were more compact and simpler to drive than the old British steam coaches of Gurney's days. The names of Bollée and Serpollet in France and Dugeon and Roper in the United States could be seen on many privately-owned steam vehicles towards the end of the century, and indeed so sophisticated were developments in method of propulsion that steam cars were produced commercially in America until after the First World War.

Steam, however, was destined to give way to a more manageable type of power. Engineers and scientists had, during the nineteenth century developed high quality metals and reliable electrical motors. Oil refining had produced petroleum spirit, and general engineering had become more accurate. These advances opened the gates to another new form of transport, the petrol-engined vehicle.

THE NEW STEAM CARRIAGE. The Guide or Engineer is seated in front, having a lever rod from the two guide wheels to turn & direct the Carriage & another at his right hand connecting with the main Steam Pipe by which he regulates the motion of the Vehicle – the hind part of the Coach contains the machinery for producing the Steam, on a novel & secure principle, which is conveyed by Pipes to the Cylinders beneath & by its action on the hind wheels sets the Carriage in motion – The Tank which contains about 60 Gallons of water is placed under the body of the Coach & is its full length and breadth – the Chimneys are fixed on the top of the hind boot & as Coke is used for fuel there will be no smoke while any hot or rarified air produced will be dispelled by the action of the Vehicle – At different stations on a journey the Coach receives fresh supplies of fuel and water – the full length of the Carriage is from 15 to 20 feet & its weight about 2 Tons – The rate of travelling is intended to be from 8 to 10 miles per hour – The present Steam Carriage carries 6 inside and 12 outside Passengers – the front Boot contains the Luggage – It has been constructed by Mr Goldsworthy Gurney, The Inventor and Patentee.

British steam coaches. **Above** *A print of Sir Goldsworth Gurney's coach of 1827.* **Opposite page, above** *The patent steam carriage designed by Sir James Anderson and W. H. James Esq (fares around 3d, speed approximately 14 mph); and* **bottom** *A coach of the early 1830s*

STEAM CARRIAGE FOR COMMON ROADS Patented July 18th, 1833, by JOHN SQUIRE and FRANCIS MACERONE of Paddington Wharf. This Carriage has run 1700 Miles & still runs every day to Edgware, Harrow or on other roads remarkable for their hills, without having required any repair. Its average speed is fourteen Miles the hour, but it has run many Miles on a level at three minutes the Mile. The cost for coke is (at London taxed price) from three pence to four pence per Mile. The horse coaches pay about three shillings per Mile for four horses more or less, according to the speed required, which never exceeds ten Miles the hour, but of which the general average is much less than eight. See the Editorial reports of 'Morning Chronicle' of Septr 3rd, Octr 7th, 14th, 15th, and 16th, 'True Sun' of Octr 5th, 'The Observer', 'Times' &c of same dates.

Gas and Gasoline

The internal combustion engine had been conceived in the seventeenth century. One of the earliest ideas was to use gunpowder to provide the explosive power, but it was not found possible to achieve continuous operation–and then the steam engine arrived.

In 1860 a Frenchman, Jean Etienne Lenoir, patented an engine like a horizontal steam engine but using coal gas. It was the first practical combustion engine; two years later he made a car with a one-and-a-half horsepower engine. It was heavy and underpowered and took an hour and a half to cover six miles, so he used it only to drive between his home and his works in Paris. He too failed to respond to opportunity's knock.

Enter Siegfried Marcus. In 1860 he rented an old building in Vienna, installed a lathe and drills and set himself up as a freelance scientist. He worked on a number of projects, among them the adaption of benzine for heating and lighting purposes. (The words petrol and gasoline were not yet in use.) This led him to invent a form of carburettor and, from this point, he began work on an internal combustion engine. He did not know about the work of Lenoir, or that which Nikolaus Otto was doing in Germany.

Security in his laboratory was Pentagon-strict. His assistants were allowed access only to parts of the engine and were never permitted to see his complete plans. Only when the engine was built did Marcus begin to consider its possible uses.

His first idea was to install it in an airship, but eventually he put it in a four-wheeled handcart. The engine was coupled directly to the back wheels, which meant they had to be lifted from the ground before the engine could be started.

One night in 1864 Marcus and his assistants pushed the contraption to a lonely lane leading to a cemetery and coaxed the engine into life. With three men aboard, the cart travelled 200 yards before breaking down. It was pushed back to the workshop where Marcus broke it up and gave little more thought to cars for several years.

The truth was that Marcus was a dilettante type of inventor, whose creative mind flitted like a butterfly from project to project, from a safety valve for steam engines to a quick-setting compound for filling cavities in teeth.

Ten years passed before he took a car on the road again. His new model was a single-cylinder four-stroke of $1\frac{1}{2}$ litres giving a top speed of five mph.

Again Marcus tested by night. One night he drove nearly eight miles, and the ring of the car's iron tyres on cobbles caused windows to be thrown open and heads to appear, complaining of the noise.

Marcus was on his third car when the police called and warned him off the public roads. He obeyed meekly. Perhaps Marcus, with his butterfly mind, did not care greatly. Perhaps he had achieved all he had set out to do; he had other projects afoot in the field of electrical development. Perhaps he realised that his slow and clumsy car had little chance of commercial viability. At any rate he confined further internal combustion development to stationary engines.

One of his cars is believed to have gone to the United States and another to the Netherlands. Their fates are unknown, but the third is in a museum in Vienna. And on a house in Malchin, a town in Mecklenburg in what is now East Germany, a plaque proclaims, 'Birthplace of Siegfried Marcus, inventor of the automobile.'

Almost certainly Marcus came nearer than any man before Benz and Daimler to establishing the new method of transport and the new way of life. He invented well, but he failed to exploit his pioneer work, like many before him, and many to come.

So today his name is little honoured outside Mecklenburg. After all the dreams that had been dreamed and all the work that had been done, it was left to Germany's Benz and Daimler to achieve the big breakthrough and to make the first cars to be available to the public.

Siegfried Marcus, who built the first petrol-driven internal combustion motor. He lived from 1831 to 1898

The Benz boys

In 1888 the Benz car was a reality and available for sale, advertised as 'an agreeable vehicle as well as a mountain-climbing apparatus'. There was only one trouble: an absence of buyers.

In August that year, Karl Benz left his home at Mannheim to attend an exhibition in Munich. His sons, Eugen, aged 15, and Richard, 13, suggested to their mother that while he was away they should borrow the car that father had built and drive to visit her family in Pforzheim, 70 miles south.

'Could you drive it?' she asked doubtfully.

'Of course,' the boys assured her. And by the first light of dawn the three of them set off, with Eugen at the tiller. It was the longest journey a motor car had ever made.

Communications were poor and few people outside Mannheim had heard of Benz's invention. Country folk crossed themselves when they saw it on its first long-distance trip. Boys threw stones, women bolted their doors and horses shied.

At Wiesloch the family halted to take on water and to buy petrol at a chemists' shop.

Along the way Eugen repaired slipping chains, blocked fuel lines and short circuits, coping manfully with each crisis as it arose. On a hill up to Bauschilott, Eugen and his mother had to get out and push, leaving Richard to steer. In the town they took on more water and Eugen cobbled new leather on to a brake.

They arrived in Pforzheim in darkness, for the car had no lights. Then they sent a telegram to Father. His first reaction was one of annoyance, but as the story of their drive spread he realised that his wife and sons had done him a great service. The news of their journey was to be worth as much to him in publicity as a Monte Carlo rally or 24-hour Le Mans race victory to a manufacturer in more recent years. For men took the view that if two schoolboys and a woman could make such a journey, then a motor must be child's play for a man. Benz began to receive orders, and to build a car a month.

His was the first car ever to be offered for sale to the public. It was also the first to be designed as a true automobile, not as a cart or horse-carriage with a motor added.

Karl Benz had thus achieved much; yet the same stubbornness that enabled him to overcome obstacles and difficulties was to prevent him from developing the car further, so that eventually he was to be almost as far behind the times as he was in front of them.

Born in 1844, the son of a German railwayman who died when Karl was only two, Benz was raised by his mother. In his own words, 'My mother set out to be both father and mother to me. She spent all she had, even her small inheritance, so that I could have a good education. She lived only for me, absolutely and completely'.

He was only 13 when he first told her, after seeing a steam engine model in his school science room, of his intention of building a vehicle to run without rails. She listened, and because she had only a meagre pension, Josephine Benz went out to work as a cook to pay for Benz's further education at a polytechnic, where he studied mathematics and engine design – which then meant, of course, steam engine design. Sadly, she died in 1870 without seeing her sacrifices repaid by Benz' success.

After leaving college, Benz worked as a mechanic in a locomotive works, starting at six am,

11

finishing at seven pm, slogging with a hammer at an anvil. His spare time he spent studying theoretical mechanics. Then, in 1871, he opened his own workshops in Mannheim to make machine parts. He took a wife, Bertha. A few years later he was penniless. The business had failed and was auctioned off. And so he turned again to engine design, and already he was thinking in terms of an engine for a road vehicle.

Nikolaus Otto had just patented a four-stroke gas engine and so, without paying licence fees to Otto, Benz was limited to work on two-strokes. His first engine ran for the first time on New Year's Eve 1879. Karl Benz himself has recorded the events that led up to the great moment. He writes:

After supper my wife said 'Let's go over to the shop and try our luck once more. Something tells me to go and it will not let me be'. So there we were, back again, standing in front of the engine as if it were a great mystery that was impossible to solve. My heart was pounding. I turned the crank.

The engine started to go 'put-put-put' and music of the future sounded with regular rhythm. We both listened to it for a full hour, fascinated, never tiring of the single note of its song. The two-cycle engine was performing as no magic flute in the world ever had. The longer it played its note the more sorrow and anxiety it conjured away from the heart . . . Suddenly the bells began to ring – New Year's Eve Bells. We felt that they were not only ringing in a new year, but a new era, which was to take on a new heartbeat from the all-important new uses of the engine.

Patent No. DRP 37435

Benz found backers and began manufacturing coal-gas engines, but he knew they were too unwieldy to be successful in cars, and when Otto's patent lapsed he went to work on a four-stroke petrol engine. This caused a breach with his less far-seeing backers. When he announced in 1884 that he was planning to concentrate all his efforts on building a car with a petrol engine a meeting with them broke up in disorder.

But Benz went ahead. First came the engine, a single-cylinder $\frac{3}{4}$ hp unit with a surface carburettor – in practice, a can stuffed with cotton wool – and a giant flywheel, mounted parallel to the ground because he thought a vertical flywheel would unbalance the vehicle. The most advanced features of it were the electric coil ignition and the world's first sparking plug.

He first tried using a direct current dynamo, the voltage of which had been increased by an induction coil to such an extent that a spark sprang between insulated platinum wire ends in the combustion chamber. 'After many wearisome trials however, it became evident that the small dynamos of those days were not fit for the work I wanted them to do,' he wrote later.

Benz switched to a battery. 'The current of the battery was of course too weak to produce a powerful igniting spark in the engine cylinder. I therefore increased the voltage of the battery current with the aid of an induction coil, just as I had the igniting current in the dynamo'.

He claimed the engine gave 250 revolutions per minute, but when it was tested after his death it was found that he had been over-modest for it reached 400 rpm. This was typical of Benz, who was never guilty of over-statement.

At this point Benz might have been expected to install the engine in a cart or tricycle as other pioneers had done, but he set out to create a real car – the first real car – planning the gearbox, steering, weight distribution, cooling and other factors from the start. At first it was going to be a four-wheeler but he was not certain that the steering would be satisfactory, so he created a three-wheeler with large rear wheels and a smaller front wheel steered by a tiller.

The car looked like a heavy bathchair with wire wheels and solid tyres. It had a steel tube frame as its chassis, to which Benz fitted a board on which was screwed the engine, where it could be reached from all sides.

The front wheel was unsprung, but there were full elliptic springs at the rear. Power was transmitted by chains to two sprockets connected to the rear axle, which had a primitive differential arrangement.

To be able to stop the car with the engine running, Benz mounted two pulleys on a countershaft, one rigidly connected to the shaft while the other turned freely. To disengage the drive he pushed aside a rod which moved the driving belt from the fixed pulley to the idler pulley, so that the engine ran without moving the wheels.

Late in 1885, the car stood in the courtyard of his workshop in Mannheim. Benz was 'proud as a king to see finally the dream of my youth standing before me,' but his first attempt at driving it ended with a crash into a wall as he missed the gateway, and the car was damaged.

After repairs and more cautious experiments he took the car on to the road. On its first trip it covered 100 metres before having to be pushed back to the workshops. And many trips ended that way.

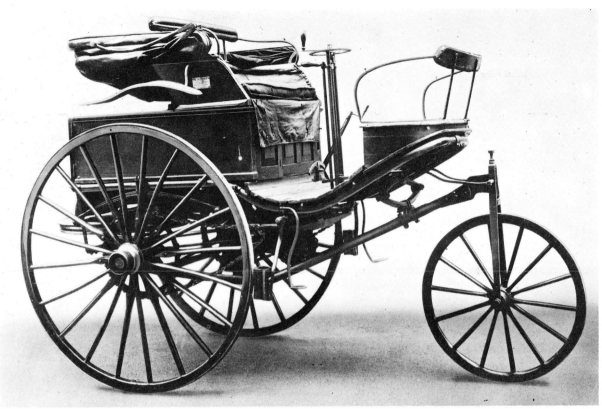

The boxy, angular Benz three-wheeler of 1888

Benz adopted the four-wheel system as soon as he had patented 'a steering mechanism for a car with steering circles set on a tangent to the wheels.' In 1893

he called his first four-wheel model Viktoria to celebrate his triumph over steering problems

Happily I did not lose courage, particularly as I noticed I was slowly progressing, he wrote.

After several weeks of attempts at driving, which aroused the astonishment of the Mannheim citizens and made me the laughing stock of passers-by, the results were satisfactory. The 100 metres become 1000 and even more, so that I could now try to drive from one town to another.

With my little car I may have reached 10 mph and very often I succeeded in conquering its caprices without being obliged to return with the help of a couple of horses or cows. My confidence was strengthened with every trip. Each time I came to know another of my vehicle's whims, and at the same time, each trip provided new suggestions for improvements, so that in January 1886 I was in a position to apply for a patent.

Press Interest

The daily newspaper 'Neue Badische Landes-zeitung' broke the news of the car in June, 1886. It was not front page news but a paragraph buried in a miscellany column, yet it declared with absolute truth, 'The wheels of automobilism have been set in motion.'

Benz went on with his trials. One newspaper report said, 'Seldom if ever have passers-by in the streets of our city seen a more startling sight than on Saturday afternoon when a one-horse chaise came down Herzog-Wilhelmstrasse at a good clip without any horse, a gentleman sitting under a surrey top and riding on three wheels— one in front and two behind—speeding on his way towards the centre of the town. The amazement of all in the street who saw him was such that they seemed unable to grasp what was before their eyes, and the astonishment was general'.

In September, 1886, the Mannheim paper 'Generalanzeiger' reported,
The difficult task of inventing may now be considered at an end and Benz intends to proceed with the making of these vehicles for practical use. This motor vehicle is not meant to have the same purpose and characteristics as a velocipede which one could take for a pleasurable spin over a smooth, well-kept country road; rather it is conceived as a cart or peasant's wagon, suitable not only for travelling fairly good roads but also for carrying heavy loads up steep inclines. For example, it would enable a commercial traveller to take his samples from one place to another without difficulty.

We believe the wagon has a good future. When the speed is made sufficient it will be the cheapest promotional tool for travelling salesmen as well as a means for tourists to get around.

One day the police called to threaten him with arrest if he drove through Mannheim again. But Benz did not knuckle under as Marcus had done years earlier in Vienna. Benz asked the Minister of the Interior of the Grand Duchy of Baden to over-rule the police—and he did; Benz was permitted to go on driving so long as he observed a speed limit of four mph in town and seven mph in the country. This did not satisfy Benz for long.

He invited the Minister to accompany him on a drive. The story is told that before they set out Benz had a private word with a milkman driving a horse-and-float. Soon after Benz had motored off the milkman overtook him, jeering at his slow progress and calling, 'Can't you go any faster?'

The Minister found the milkman's insults intolerable. 'Really, Herr Benz,' he protested, 'Can't we go faster than this?'

'Easily,' replied Benz, 'but your regulations don't allow it.'

And, according to the story, the Minister retorted, 'Damn the regulations!' and the speed limit was as good as buried.

It was shortly after this incident that Benz's sons made their dramatic drive; soon Benz had 50 men working for him and was exporting his cars to England and America. This was the car:

Engine	
Number of cylinders	one
Arrangement	horizontal
Bore	91·4 mm
Stroke	150 mm
Capacity	985 cc
Ignition	high tension electric
Method of operation	slider, exhaust through valve
Carburettor	own-make surface carburettor
Cooling	by water evaporation
Output	0·88 hp at 400 rpm
Transmission	belt and chains
Steering	rack and steering lever
Brake	band brake acting on countershaft
Chassis	
Frame	steel tubing with four cross-members
Wheels	solid rubber tyres on steel-spoked wheels
Front wheel diameter	730 mm
Rear wheel diameter	1125 mm
Track	1190 mm
Wheelbase	1450 mm
Springs	front unsprung, rear fully elliptic
Weight of car	265 kg
Overall length	2378 mm

But Benz's backers were still not sold on cars. 'You will ruin us,' they said and withdrew their support. By 1890 Karl had found new partners, Friedrich von Fischer and Julius Ganss, and began work on an improved steering arrangement with a four-wheel car in mind. The new car had a three hp engine, belt-and-pulley gears for 'fast driving' or 'hill driving' and the direction was changed by 'a mechanism with steering circles set on a tangent to the wheels.' The car represented a big stride towards an entirely new model based on more advanced mechanics. Karl Benz called it the 'Viktoria', not after the English Queen, but after the German Empress, and perhaps to celebrate his victory over technical problems.

First small car

The Viktoria led in 1894 to the Velo. Benz, with his customary modesty made no exaggerated claims for it, yet it was the world's first small car, the first standard production car and the first step towards the 'people's car' which was to be the goal of car makers all over the world.

Originally the Velo was equipped with a $1\frac{1}{2}$ hp engine, but later a $2\frac{3}{4}$ hp engine was used and the car became known as the Comfortable. A third speed reduction, the 'mountain gear' was also added.

Not only in Germany did Benz's small car cause a sensation, but also in France, England and the USA, reaching a sales figure quite unusual at that time. According to an 1896 prospectus, this vehicle 'could master gradients up to one in ten on good roads,' and cost '2000 marks, complete with the best of equipment and lamps.'

Benz sold 67 cars in 1894 and 135 the next year.

In 1894 Benz offered the Velo to the public – the first deliberately small car, and a first step towards a 'people's car'

Karl Benz, November 25, 1844 – April 4, 1929

He sold 256 in 1897 and 434 in 1898. Sales rose steadily to a peak 603 in 1900, by which time he had produced more than 2000 cars. But in 1901 his production dropped to 385. By 1903 sales were down to 172.

The simple truth was that, like the Wright brothers in aviation, Benz failed to maintain his lead. He had retained his surface carburettor, his tiller steering and his basic engine design too long. The changes he had made were too slight, too few and too late, and by the turn of the century the Benz was slow compared with Daimler-engined cars. The race-bred Mercedes spelt the beginning of the end.

Benz's partners turned on him for his stubbornness, and called in French engineer Marius Barbarou, to design new models. Benz was resentful and walked out of the firm in 1903, though he returned a year later.

But the genius and perseverance of Karl Benz was not to be ignored or forgotten. Five years after the great Daimler-Benz merger had begun and the 85-year-old 'father of the motor car' lay bed-ridden in his home, a motorcade of vehicles from all over Germany paraded past his house in an Easter salute with the slogan 'Do Honour to Your Master', and a flight of Baden Flying Club planes dropped a victor's wreath near his Villa Benz. A few days later, on April 4, 1929, Karl Benz died.

A gift for Frau Daimler

April 29 1886, was Emma Daimler's 43rd birthday, and her husband had ordered a birthday present for her. It was a coach, designed to be pulled by a horse, and Gottlieb Daimler had given instructions to the makers in Stuttgart that it should be 'handsomely but solidly built'. He had also instructed that, as it was to be a surprise present, it should be delivered to his home at Canstatt after dark.

So it was. But when the coach arrived, Daimler removed the shafts. He then installed steering gear and put an engine of his own design between the front and rear seats. For while it was, in a sense, a surprise gift for Frau Daimler, he was more concerned with secrecy for other reasons: the coach was to become the first Daimler car.

It was, in fact, to become the first successful four-wheel petrol-engined car, though Daimler was in no way trying to rival Karl Benz who, at that time, had just made his three-wheeler. For the astonishing fact was that Daimler knew nothing about Benz's work at Mannheim, 60 miles away, and even more astonishingly the two were never to meet.

Daimler's car incorporated, even at this early stage, ideas that were to be hailed as inspired innovations when re-introduced by others years later. For instance, the engine was mounted on rubber to dampen shock and vibration. It also had fan cooling (replaced later by a finned water radiator) and pre-heating of the gas-air mixture by exhaust gas.

It had a friction clutch of advanced design that gripped well and disengaged faultlessly. The two-speed gearbox used disengageable belt pulleys. The differential gear, assuring compensation between the two road wheels running at different speeds on bends, used flexible leather washers fitted into the hollow body of a pinion.

Like Benz, Daimler tried out his car first in his yard, then took it out on the roads, where it reached 11 mph.

Frau Daimler's present was an important and original one. But it was to be another three years before Daimler went into production with a car. He had not set out to design a car as Benz had, but rather to add power to a coach, as he had already done to a bicycle, and was about to do to a boat.

But although Daimler's first car was not in the Benz class, he had produced a more efficiently-designed engine than Benz, the first to operate at reasonably high revolutions, and the forerunner of all internal-combustion car engines to follow.

Engine	
Number of cylinders	one
Arrangement of	vertical
Bore	70 mm
Stroke	120 mm
Piston displacement	0·46 litres
Ignition	hot tube
Output	1·5 hp at 700 rpm
Control	Four-stroke
Arrangement of valves	vertical
Intake valve	automatic
Exhaust valve	controlled by cam disc via push-pull rod
Cooling	air-blower (later water)
Transmission	
Clutch	friction clutch
Gearbox	two-speed belt
Drive	pinion and ring gear
Control	swivelling bolster
Brakes	external shoe on wheel rim, linkage
Chassis	
Wheels	wood, reinforced with iron
Tread	1250 mm
Wheelbase	1340 mm
Total weight	495 kg

1886: Daimler rides in the passenger seat of his first automobile, driven by his son Adolf

Below *Built in 1885 and patented on January 29, 1886: Karl Benz's first car, 'propelled by a gas engine,' by which he meant an 'engine driven by fuel which consists of gas vapourised from a liquid by means of an apparatus carried on the vehicle'*
Right *Founder Karl Benz drives his first car again at Munich in 1925*

Born in 1834 in Schorndorf, Württemberg, where his father, who had originally owned a bakery and wine bar, later became the town's chief architect, Daimler was apprenticed at 14 to a gunsmith. At 19 he began work in a locomotive factory, went on to Stuttgart Polytechnic Institute, then in 1861 travelled to England to work in machine and tool factories in Leeds, Manchester and Coventry. Returning to Germany, he became manager in 1863 of an engineering works making locomotives, bridges and machinery for paper mills.

It was in this factory that Daimler met Wilhelm Maybach, 12 years his junior; a carpenter's son who had been orphaned at the age of 10. It was the start of a lifelong association.

In 1867, newly married to Emma, a chemist's daughter, Daimler saw an Otto gas engine at a Paris exposition; five years later he joined the Otto and Langen company, *Gasmotoren-Fabrik Deutz,* as factory manager, and took Maybach with him as chief designer.

Daimler took charge of what was a small handbuilt operation and built it up by volume methods. In 1875 a staff of 230 built and delivered 634 engines to customers.

But Daimler was well aware of the limitations of gas engines, big, cumbersome and lacking in power. And that year he initiated work on petrol engines with slide-controlled flame ignition. Two years later he experimented unsuccessfully with electric ignition.

By 1882 he and Otto had begun to disagree about the future of the firm and so Daimler resigned and set up on his own at Canstatt, taking Maybach with him. They acquired a villa on the edge of a park, turned a garden toolshed into an office and part of the house into a workshop. In 1883 they began to build stationary petrol engines.

Benz had been ahead of his time with electric ignition but had not been able to make it particularly efficient. Daimler patented hot tube ignition, which was more primitive, but which worked well. It involved a platinum tube which projected into the cylinder. Kept red hot by a Bunsen type of burner, it carried the heat into the combustion chamber and ignited the petrol vapour. Daimler wrote:

It was a long road, requiring endless tests and unremitting pursuit of the objective. Premature firing of the mixture occurred again and again, when the flywheel was suddenly and unexpectedly thrown backwards instead of forwards, and the crank would be ripped out of the technician's hand like a bolt of lightning.

In this workshop, in the small German town of Bad Canstatt, Gottlieb Daimler produced his motor cycle (1885), his first motor car, and his first motor boat (both 1886)

But in the end it worked, and worked well, and was to be used by Daimler until 1897 when he adopted the electric ignition system devised by Robert Bosch.

It gave the Daimler engine higher speeds – up to 800 rpm – than had ever been known; the engine itself was also lighter and smaller than any earlier petrol engine.

By 1885 Daimler and Maybach were selling their engines for use with fire pumps and printing presses. Then, as Benz completed his three-wheeler, Daimler produced his motorcycle. There were few bicycles on the roads at this time; the penny farthing with its outsize front wheel and small rear one had only just yielded to the 'safety' model with equal-sized wheels. Daimler's motor bicycle also had wooden wheels of equal diameter, shod with iron tyres; it had handlebars like a bathchair and a $\frac{1}{2}$ hp motor fitted under a horse-type saddle. There was a surface carburettor, fan cooling and belt drive to the rear wheel arranged to provide two speeds. The brake was operated by a cord.

Road trials were carried out mainly after dark, as had been those of earlier pioneers like Murdock and Marcus. They were handled by Paul Daimler, Gottlieb's 17-year-old eldest son. On November 10 1885 he rode to Untertürkheim, nearly two miles and back. With a skid in place of the front wheel he also rode on a frozen lake.

But the motor car was to come before the motorcycle, for Daimler switched his ideas to a four-wheeler. And Frau Daimler's birthday present was ordered.

The automobile had claimed Gottlieb Daimler's first attention but was not alone the object of his plans. The power unit was the core of his exertions: he saw a great many uses within reach now. After road vehicles, water craft, rail transport – everything was to be motorised. Later his engine would be adapted for aeronautical uses. Daimler dreamed – and set the wheels of concrete achievement in motion.

In 1886 Daimler built the world's first motor boat. For security reasons he dressed the sides of the boat with insulators and wires to suggest it was electric powered. A local paper reported:
Recently a boat has been circulating on the Neckar with about eight persons on board. It appears to be propelled by some unseen power up and down-stream with great speed, causing astonishment to bystanders. The little ship has been fitted out with special propelling mechanism by engineer Daimler. The man at the tiller needs only to press in one direction or another to have the boat go anywhere he wants, either quickly or slowly.

Daimler and Maybach moved to larger premises, and began work on a two-cylinder V-engine, one with a considerably reduced power-to-weight ratio. About this time Daimler heard of a dirigible balloon flight in Germany, and, fired by his dream of aero-power, fitted and installed a single-cylinder engine, gearing it to two air screws, one for lift and one for thrust. In 1888 this balloon made a highly successful $2\frac{1}{2}$-mile-hop from Seelberg to Kornwestheim.

continued on page 22

Daimler's motor boat on the river Neckar near Canstatt. At first he disguised it with wires and insulators to suggest electric motive power

Above *A Zeppelin ancestor: the single-cylinder Daimler engine, geared to two screws, one for thrust and one for lift, which proved highly successful in 1888, when the dirigible to which this ensemble was attached made a flight of 2½ miles from the Daimler factory at Seelberg and* **right** *'. . . rented by the week, month or year . . . for doctors, travellers, etc.' A hire-car advertisment, circa 1895*

Below *High fashion in Berlin's Grunewald: a Daimler taxi of 1899*

The Benz Velo of 1895—the first standard production small car, and a step towards a popular car

The first 35 hp Mercedes were succeeded by the Mercedes-Simplex series; this is the 40 hp model of 1902

continued from page 19

Finally in 1888, the year in which his wife died, Daimler designed at last a real car, a two-seater with four speeds and a tubular frame through which coolant circulated.

He showed it at the Paris World Fair. The public were not excited, any more than they were by Benz's car, but it interested Emile Levassor and René Panhard, who ran a French factory making engines for sawmills . . .

Meanwhile, William Steinway, the American piano manufacturer, had acquired the rights to Daimler engines in the USA, and a young English engineer named Frederick Simms had won the British rights.

England's Daimler company, today the prestige marque of the British Leyland Motor Corporation, began making cars in Coventry in 1896, using the Daimler patents. And so the Daimler engine designs conquered the early motoring world.

Daimler's most successful car was still to come. In 1897 Emil Jellinek, an Austrian race driver living in Nice, began to sell Daimler cars in the South of France. He saw that many race winners used Daimler engines but preferred Panhard-Levassor vehicles.

Jellinek persuaded Daimler to design a six hp racing car. It was too slow to be competitive. A year later Daimler made a $7\frac{1}{4}$ hp car which led to a racing two-seater with a four-cylinder 28 hp engine. That was almost too fast. It weighed two tons, had questionable handling and could be dangerous; in 1900 works driver Wilhelm Bauer was killed at the wheel of one.

Jellinek urged Daimler to make the car longer and lower. 'Do this,' he said, 'and I will take 36 cars to sell.' At the same time he proposed

A Daimler belt-driven car, pictured in England in 1896, the year the 4 mph speed limit had been lifted.

King Edward VII was given a ride in this model — and Britain joined the motoring era

a new name, which would, he said, help the cars to sell in France. The name was that of his 11-year-old daughter, Mercedes.

Daimler was 66 and ill, and the bulk of the design work on the new car fell to the faithful Maybach, but the new Mercedes, with a four-cylinder engine giving 35 hp, made its debut in 1900 and the following year it distinguished itself in the Nice race week.

It was to win many international races and to establish itself as the most successful car of its time. But Daimler did not live to see its triumph. He died in March 1900.

And Maybach? He left the firm in 1907 to design aircraft engines for Zeppelins, dying in 1929.

Gottlieb's son, Paul Daimler, carried on the firm that had been started by one of the most productive partnerships in history.

Top *Mercedes Jellinek, whose name was to have more sales-appeal than 'Daimler'*
Above *The first Mercedes, with a 35 hp, 4-cylinder engine*
Left *Nice Week 1901; the new 35 mph Mercedes won everything in sight*

Commemoration run

Today, November 14 1896, is a red-letter day, not only in the history of automobilism, but in that of England itself, for it marks the throwing open of the highways and byways of our beautiful country to those who elect to travel thereupon in carriages propelled by motors . . .

So said the jubilant 'Autocar' on that great day when the first run from London to Brighton to mark the emancipation of the car and the repeal of the 'Red Flag' Act was made. It was indeed an historic day in the story of motoring – and it is surprising that no attempt was made to repeat it until 32 years later – in November 1928, when a Commemoration Run was sponsored by the 'Autocar' and two newspapers. Since then it has been held every year (with the exception of a seven-year break during World War 2) and today it is estimated that around three million spectators line the route to watch the 250 or so ancient and valuable motor cars trundle and clank their smoky way to the sea . . .

continued on page 28

Right *An 1897 Daimler Tonneau (2-cylinder, 4 hp) passes London's Big Ben at the Houses of Parliament on its way to the sea on the annual rally to commemorate the Emancipation Run of 1896, and* **above** *an 1897 Benz reaches Brighton*
Opposite page
The Clément-Talbot company was formed to market Clément automobiles in Britain, and for a year cars sold in that country were called Clement-Talbots. At the end of 1903 the name became plain Talbot

24

Right *A Mercedes six-seater limousine of 1903*
Below *A family car for the very rich: the 6 litre Mercedes with bodywork by Farina, 1926*
Bottom *The Mercedes 24/100/140 hp was re-designed when the companies of Mercedes and Benz amalgamated in 1926, and was brought out as the model 'K'. The 6·25 litre engine developed 160 hp when supercharged. From this car came the famous 'SS' and 'SSK' models, with engines of 7·1 litres. This is an 'SS' cabriolet of 1928*

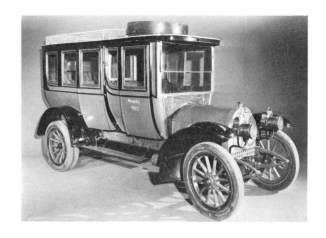

A licence for Madame Sarazin

In 1886, René Panhard and Emile Levassor were operating a wood-working machinery company in Paris. About this time, Edouard Sarazin, a lawyer friend of Levassor's, acquired the rights to produce Daimler engines in Belgium and France. Unfortunately, he died the following year. A little later, Mme Sarazin married Emile Levassor; with her hand in marriage went the Daimler licence, and with the licence, the company of Panhard & Levassor entered the motor manufacturing world, and laid the foundation-stone of the French motor industry. So when the company of Panhard & Levassor started producing engines under Daimler licence in 1889, the factors leading up to this significant event in motoring history had been somewhat domestic in origin!

In 1890 the manufacture of automobile engines was entirely separate from that of the vehicle's bodywork, and the normal routine was to put the automotive unit inside a coach or similar body and hope for the best.

Levassor decided to build an automobile without reference to horse-drawn traditions. He built a cabriolet with the Daimler V-twin power unit installed in the centre of the vehicle – and uncomfortably close to the passengers' backs. In February 1891, says the company's notebook: 'With Levassor piloting, it effected without incident, a voyage to Ivry-Boulogne and back. Fifteen days later Levassor pushed with success around Versailles.' We trust that 'pushed' (pousse) was idiomatic for 'drive' at the time . . .

Levassor was not happy with the midships
continued on page 30

In 1890, Emile Levassor built a car powered by a Daimler V-twin engine mounted between the passengers, who sat back-to-back

Left to right: René Panhard, Madame Levassor (formerly Sarazin), Emile Levassor and engineer Mayarde

continued from page 25

Back-seat drivers? This 1902 De Dion-Bouton is listed as a cab, but it looks like a self-drive hire-car here

Opposite page, above left *A 1904 Cadillac chugs up an incline amid modern traffic on the London to Brighton road. This is a 1-cylinder tourer developing 8½ hp. The American Cadillac company was just one year old when this model was built* **Above right** *Alexander Winton of Cleveland formed his company in 1897 and recorded 37·7 mph in his 12 hp experimental car that year. This is a Winton of 1903, with a 2-cylinder horizontally-opposed engine.* **Bottom** *A 1904 De Dion-Bouton*

continued from page 27

engine and played about with the layout for a while, finally deciding on a front-engined design for the Mark 2. It became known as 'Le Système Panhard' and was virtually the first modern automobile layout. The rest of the car was rather thrown together. The motor drove through a friction clutch and a gearbox with its gearwheels in the open air, and a rough tiller, and heavy, boxy, coachwork. Said Emile of this first model *C'est brusque et brutal, mais ça marche.* 'It's rough and brutish, but it goes'. This is how the official story of the company tells of vehicle No. 2 and its maiden voyage:

*En Juin 1891, une seconde voiture est prête. . . .
Levassor la conduit, fin Juillet, jusqu'à Etretat et en
revient sans trop de problèmes. Moyenne générale :
10 km/h, avec des pointes à 17 km/h, malgré 'une
gazoline faisant mauvais effet dans les brûleurs'.*
(A second car was ready in June 1891 . . .
Levassor drove it as far as Etretat at the end of July and got home again without much trouble. His average was 10 km/h, sometimes touching 17 km/h, in spite of 'petrol that did no good to the sparking plugs'.)

Levassor was acquainted with a Monsieur Armand Peugeot, whose family owned a large ironmongery company. Armand had already dabbled in steam cars, with the eminent Serpollet, and was soon convinced by Emile Levassor that the Daimler motors were an efficient and functional proposition. By 1891 he had his first Peugeot-Levassor on the road with its Daimler V unit rear-mounted in a two-seater quadricycle. (This was, in fact, the spur that prodded Levassor into building complete cars under his own company's name – previously the engines had been sold as stationary units). A Peugeot four-seater followed (no less than 64 were made, a huge number for that date) and in 1892 a *vis-à-vis* with a large Daimler V twin.

Thus 'Les Fils de Peugeot Frères', the Sons of Peugeot Brothers, a company with a name like a film title, became the first French motor manufacturers to sell a commercially-produced car in France. Five were sold in 1891.

Armand Peugeot had a bright idea worthy of a modern public relations man when he entered one of his cars in the 1891 Paris-Brest race – an event for bicycles! His car completed the trip at an average of around 10 miles an hour and was soundly beaten by the cyclists. But a Peugeot had made the first genuine long-distance journey and Armand had made news that was to boost sales significantly.

When France inaugurated its first motor

Emile Levassor, one-time mining engineer, and designer and builder of the car that set the pattern for automobile layout for many years

René Panhard, born 1841, former head of a wood-working company, became, in association with Emile Levassor, joint chief of the great French motor company

This neat quadricycle, Armand Peugeot's Type A, was entered in the 1891 Paris-Brest bicycle race as an observer vehicle

sport event in 1894 and started a programme of frequent races soon afterwards (which are described and illustrated in the later chapter 'The first races'), it put the country and its automobile industry ahead of the rest of the world—even ahead of the German manufacturers who had, after all, started the whole business but who, at this point in time, were suffering financial and policy difficulties.

Both Panhard & Levassor and Peugeot entered the lists of competition, and raced regularly for several years. The first Grand Prix took place in France, and the new motor sport was nurtured there in those early motoring days. Because of the French lead in those pioneering days the 'official' language of motor racing is French (just as Italian is accepted in music) and the French Grand Prix is still the 'classic' Formula 1 race of the motor sport calendar.

Other French manufacturers entered the field as soon as their designers could get something down on the drawing board. Amédée Bollée, successful steam car maker, had filed a patent for an internal combustion motor by 1894 and two years later had built a small four-wheeled vis-à-vis with a 2-cylinder petrol engine, and a number of features advanced enough to interest other would-be manufacturers two of whom

Amédée Bollée, 1867–1926

continued on page 34

Early Peugeots. **Below left** *is a vis-á-vis, with canopy, of 1892. This had a 2-cylinder motor of 1645 cc and a claimed maximum speed of 30 km/h Two years later – the year of the first motor sport event – Peugeot offered the handsome brake (**below, right**) to the public. With 5 seats and a V-twin Daimler engine, it was designed as a family vehicle*

and **bottom** *as raced in the 1894 Paris to Rouen event: an 1894 Peugeot*

Opposite page *Canstatt-Daimler, 1899, with the 23 hp 4-cylinder Phoenix engine. This car, which could be called the prototype of the Mercedes, was built for Count Zborowski*

Following Panhard and Levassor's success, other French industrial producers turned to motor manufacture. Early on the scene was Emile Delahaye, who owned a brick-making machinery company. The first Delahaye *used a Benz-type motor placed at the rear. This is the 1896 model; note the hunting horn in the co-driver's hand!*

continued from page 31
took out licences to build the Bollée design. A few years later several new marques, some remembered with affection, some with respect, some not at all, began to appear on the French market—Renault, Mors (then fast becoming a motor racing leader), Delahaye (early models based on Benz principles), Darracq (first car 1895, born in Alexandre Darracq's cycle-parts works in Suresness), Decauville (racing as early as 1898), De Dion-Bouton (partnership of the aristo, Marquis de Dion, and his employee Georges Bouton; took out first patents for a 'detonating motor cooled by water' in 1889), Gobron Brillié (with its opposed-pistons engine in which each cylinder contained two pistons), then lesser-known names such as Rochet (1899–1905), Omega (1900), Manon (1903–1905), Ader (1900–1907), Allard-Latour (1899–1902), Bonneville (1897–1900), Bourguignonne (1899–1901), Gautier (1902–1903), and literally hundreds of other long-forgotten marques that briefly bloomed and perished.

Panhard and Levassor produced this front-engined commercial vehicle – claimed to be the first in the world – in 1895

34

Into the new century and the sophistication of weather protection: Peugeot's 1906 Torpedo open touring car.

Four cylinders, 12 hp, four-speed gearbox plus reverse, chain transmission

French 'Voiture sans cheval' elegance: a 6 hp Peugeot 3/4 coupé, made between 1898 and 1901 at Audincourt. This model has rarity value—only two were made

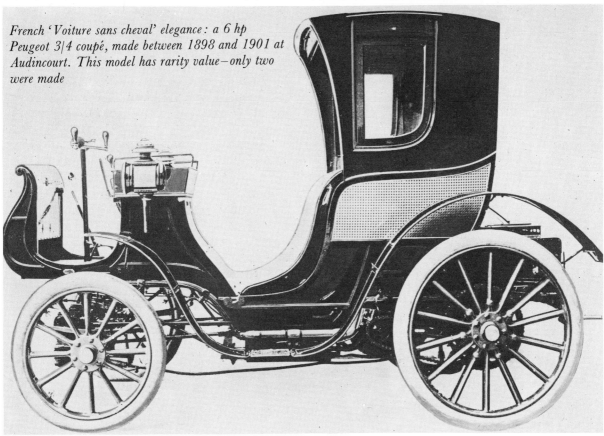

The red flag falls

The year is 1895; the place, an urban road in England. A top-hatted man walks smartly down the road, holding aloft a small red flag. He appears to be quite alone. A moment later one can hear the tuff-tuff-tuff of a small engine from around a curve in the road obscured by a high country hedge.

A full 60 yards behind Top-hat trundles a squarish horseless carriage, the name Panhard Levassor inscribed on its box-like front. One person is steering its long tiller, another sits alongside him, looking rather unhappy. Two passengers sit on the rear seat, facing the direction from which the vehicle has come. The speed of the carriage is approximately 4 mph.

The law of the land has stated that such self-propelled vehicles as may dare to use the roads shall not exceed that of the flagman. It is difficult to understand the purpose of the vehicle; a team of horses would do so much more for the travellers in much less time and much more comfort.

And this scene was enacted in Britain (not often it must be admitted, for few were so foolhardy as to purchase a horseless carriage in 1895) whilst Emile Levassor was winning the 732 miles Paris-Bordeaux-Paris race, and the motor industry in Europe was fast establishing its commercial future.

In 1895 there was virtually no automobile industry in Britain. The horse had held sway since time immemorial, and the land-owners liked it that way. The state of the roads and the numbers of vehicles that used them had been of some concern to the authorities both national and regional since earlier in the nineteenth century, when they had decided that steam vehicles were a device of the devil.

Acts of Parliament had been passed over the years since the steam coach first made its unwelcome appearance on the highways of England, legislation that hog-tied any vehicles other than those drawn by the good old horse. **Be it enacted by the Queen's most excellent Majesty.** The 1861 Act began in the traditionally grandiloquent way, **by and with the advice of the Lords Spiritual and Temporal** (which seemed to indicate that the Archbishop of Canterbury was also interested) **an Act to Regulate the use of Locomotives on Highways** and gets to the meat of the

document by pin-pointing **every locomotive propelled by its own power, containing within itself the machinery for its own propulsion** and setting out fees for the use by steam coaches of the ubiquitous toll roads of the country. Self-propelled vehicles were taxed at a rate at which every two tons (and they were all over that weight) were as one horse-and-cart. Heavier weights drew crushing fees for crossing artificial lines such as county boundaries. For exceeding the speed limit of ten miles an hour in the countryside and five through villages and towns the fine was a cracking £5.

Lights were also made necessary by this Act. **The person in charge of the locomotive shall provide two efficient lights one on each side of same between the hours of one hour after sunset and one hour before sunrise.** Things haven't changed much in some respects.

Four years later, another Act was passed in Britain; this time authority used its teeth in an even more effective way. Said this notorious 'Red Flag' Act: **Firstly at least three people shall be employed to drive or conduct such a locomotive ... Secondly that one of such persons, while any locomotive is in motion, shall precede such locomotive on foot by not less than sixty yards, and shall carry a red flag constantly displayed, and shall warn riders and drivers of horses of the approach of such locomotives and shall signal the driver thereof when it shall be necessary to stop ... Fifthly every such locomotive shall be stopped by any person with a horse or carriage drawn by a horse by putting up his hand.** Speed limits for self-propelled vehicles were here reduced to four miles an hour—and to two through built-up regions.

This Act, far from being concerned with safety (although it must be admitted that steam coaches made an unholy noise and showered sparks all over the nice clean countryside) was intended to halt the progress and development of machine-driven transport. It succeeded, and in 1865 mechanised road transport came to a hissing, grinding halt.

That suffocating Act of Parliament was the sole reason for Britain's painfully slow entry into the world of the automobile. For it stayed on the

London-to-Brighton Run, 1896, when the shackles were struck off for British motorists. The scene at the   *Hotel Metropole in London at the start, with a distinguished company of 'automobilists' ready to go . . .*

. . . and eager crowds swarming round the London-Brighton cars during their stop at the White Hart Hotel in Reigate, Surrey

Statute Books down to 1896, when Europe and the United States had been tinkering away for over a decade at the spidery machines that were soon to change the face of the world.

There was much agitation by influential people for many years, but motoring, if it could be so called at this early date, continued to be impracticable, if not effectively illegal, until the repeal of the 1865 Act.

Some time around 1895, Britain woke up to the fact that horses were old-hat and the smart carriage was one without a nag in the shafts. In Germany and France both motor cars and motor cycles were being produced in commercial numbers, and in America the brothers Duryea had set up in business, though their first effort was more of a buggy with an engine fitted to it than a true motor-car such as the Europeans were turning out.

Not that British inventors were unaware of the turn of events. Back in 1884 one Edward Butler had taken out a patent for 'the mechanical propulsion of cycles' and by 1888 had built a

Edward Butler, a Devon farmer's son, took out a patent for 'the mechanical propulsion of bicycles' in 1884, and four years later had made this two-stroke tricycle; he drove it at 12 mph

A tricycle driven by a Lawson Motor Wheel, with two young late Victorians sharing the tiller. The motor drove only a single wheel, and could be fitted as a third wheel to two-wheeled horse-vehicles. Circa 1897

two-stroke tricycle and driven it at 12 mph. A year later this Devon farmer's boy had converted his vehicle to four-stroke, but he failed to put his early motor into commercial production, mainly due to the discouraging effect of the Red Flag Act.

James Roots had built a two-stroke tricycle, only seven years after Benz and Daimler had 'invented' the automobile, and John Henry Knight of Farnham had, in 1895, driven his 1 hp petrol-driven car–and had been fined for conducting it at 9 mph.

The great British Motorists' Charter of 1896 is found in the Statute Book lying between a Land Heritage Law and a Judicial Trustees Act. The advancement in Law represented by the other two Acts may be debatable–but the **Act to Amend the Law with Respect to the Use of Locomotives on Highways** gave birth to the British automotive industry, promoted increased communication between the people of Britain, and signalled the decline of the horse. The Act started by announcing apparently trivial changes in the law relating to lights and bells on motor cars, then stated that **No light locomotive shall travel along a public highway at a greater speed than fourteen miles an hour.** The chains that had shackled motoring in Britain had been struck off.

One of the first Humbers, 1899; a voiturette powered by a 2½ hp De Dion front-mounted engine, it had front-wheel drive and rear-wheel steering!

Five years later in 1904, Humber were making this very popular Beeston Humber light car

The New 10-12 h.p. Beeston Humber Light Car.

On 14 November 1896 the Red Flag Act was finally relegated to history. A celebration run from London to Brighton was organised, as 'The Autocar' said:

to mark the dividing line between the old and the new . . . the ride to Brighton should form a fitting, impressive, and practical commencement of the new era, which is undoubtedly destined to work so great and beneficial a revolution in the life, habits and methods of locomotion of the people of this country. Surely today should be a day of true rejoicing, and the hearts of autocarists be glad in the land.

The 'autocarists' of three-quarters of a century later may possibly have different views . . .

However, on that November morning in 1896 they tore up the hated red flag and thirty-odd 'autocarists' set course for Brighton on the south coast of England, a distance of some 53 miles.

The crowds on the route were vast; it seemed that everybody in the country had taken this abolition of the 4 mph limit as a symbol of the developing freedom that motor transport was beginning to provide, and had turned out to see

Four years after 'Emancipation Day' in 1896, the Automobile Club mounted its marathon 1000 Miles Trial round Britain, lasting 18 days. This shows a halt outside Edinburgh, northernmost point of the Trial

Early English. The textile firm of Horsfall and Bickham (who still exist) produced the Horbick Minor in 1905. This four-seater had a 3 cylinder engine and a number of advanced features – a good buy at £300

the cars, which included a number of French entries, two American Duryeas, a couple of steam bicycles, and a handful of electric vehicles, including an invalid-chair.

Emancipation Day as it was called, was the catalyst that precipitated the British car industry into bustling competition with the rest of the motor manufacturing world. Daimlers built under licence started to roll out of their Coventry works; Frederick Lanchester, to whom must go the credit for the first successful four-wheel British car, got under way around 1898; Wolseley, with Herbert Austin as designer, began producing; Humber, once known for its bicycles, showed a first four-wheel model at an 1899 show. As the reign of Queen Victoria drew to a close, the automobile gained a firm place in the daily scene in Britain, as it had a few years earlier in Europe. Men of vision, engineers and businessmen, turned their energies towards the twentieth century and the great new industry being forged in the workshops of the world.

The Iron Works at Vauxhall join the motor age: the first Vauxhall car, 1903

Wolseley, with Herbert Austin as designer, break into the passenger-service field: a Wolseley bus, 1905

The men who were mainsprings

It started as a one-man experiment in Germany, then spread to France and Britain, and the USA. Soon after the turn of the century it was the 'in' thing to own or be seen in an automobile. At least, it was if your oil-well was gushing . . .

Later came the grandes marques, some in the United States, mostly in Europe. Beautiful objects like Bugattis, Rolls-Royces, Dussenbergs, Bentleys, Hispano-Suizas, cars without which the world would have been a greyer, duller place.

They created the desire to buy mobility with elegance, and a few could afford them. But most purses could not get within the price of a set of seat-covers of these exalted gems of the motoring world. And few of us today can include those that are still with us in anything but our happiest dreams.

The grandes marques made history, but the others, the Austins, Fords, Renaults, Fiats, Opels, these *were* history. The products of these and other similar companies–and the men who created them–are part of the fabric and pattern of the daily lives of millions.

Immediately after Benz and Daimler rolled out their first shaky machines one could be excused for assuming that there might have been something of a rush to get into the horseless-carriage business on the ground floor.

No such rush materialised. There may have been a few thousand back-yarders tinkering with their bits of old gas or steam engines (mostly in the USA, where the pioneering spirit seems to be inbuilt) but there was a noticeably cool reception elsewhere. At least five years passed before interest became more widespread–with the Daimler licence-to-build inherited by Mme Sarazin, who later wed Emile Levassor.

But there were several people who had kept their eyes and their imaginations open, who had watched and learned, and searched for the right product and right moment to present it. Here, briefly are the opening moves of four of the earliest in the business–the men who were the mainsprings of the companies of Opel, Austin, Fiat, Renault . . .

Louis of France

The sound of hammering came from the garden shed of the Renault home in respectable Billancourt, a quiet suburb of Paris.

Wielder of the hammer was a tall, gangling young fellow, not too well endowed with academic ability, according to his teachers, and with, as writer André Maurois later said, the face of a poet. As a creator and innovator, Renault could almost be termed a poet; add to that his genius for empire-building, and one understands a little of how he became one of the most powerful men of his time and his country.

During his youth Renault had met Serpollet, maker of steam cars, had been taken out for an evening ride (which ended in a ditch) and had been fired with 'automobilism'. Despite Louis' lack of scholastic distinction, his father, a solid, sensible bourgeois draper, did not forbid his son's interest in the only hobby he had – and when the boy was 14 he even bought an old Panhard engine for him to tinker with.

Hence the banging in the garden shed. And it was banging to some result, as the small world of suburban Paris was to know the following year, 1898. Here Renault junior, aged 21, converted a De Dion tricycle into a Renault quadricycle by adding another road wheel. His first 'car' had a three-speed gearbox plus reverse, was quiet, flexible, and lighter than most vehicles on the roads of France.

Christmas Eve 1898: Maître Viot, a friend of Renault père, asked if he might have a ride in Louis' new voiturette. He was taken up to the Place du Tertre on the Butte Montmartre, one of the only hills in the city. Viot took out 40 gold coins, placed them on the table of the restaurant in which they were having an après-voyage drink – and became Renault's first customer. Twelve more trips were made in the car that night, twelve orders were placed for Renault voiturettes, and Louis went home with his pockets full of deposit-money.

Brothers Marcel and Fernand joined Louis in the new business, and on February 25 1899 Renault Frères was formed.

Within six months, the Renault company had sold 60 voiturettes, and had produced the world's first saloon car.

Renault cars soon proved themselves in motor races. The town-to-town races of the day were frequent, and the Renault brothers were quick to see that a victory could be strong sales promotion. Paris-Trouville, Paris-Ostend, Paris-Rambouillet, all recorded Renault voiturettes in the winners' lists.

In 1901, a 745-mile race from Paris to Berlin marked the beginning to the capital-to-capital races of that era. A field of 109 was subjected to stringent rules and the race promised to be a no-quarter-given contest. The French Press called it the 'madman's race' but was loud in its praises when the three winners were announced – a French Mors in the heavy class, a Panhard-Levassor in the light, and Louis Renault in the voiturette class. The first German car, a Mercedes, was placed 18th, behind 17 French vehicles. One may imagine with what verve the French National Anthem was played on their return home . . .

The Paris-Vienna race of 1902 was the high-point of them all. By this time motor racing had begun to attract great crowds and some 10,000 spectators gathered to see the start at Paris. With 117 cars and 1050 miles to go, it was to be run in four sections and three classes. Marcel and Louis Renault were entered in their small 4 cylinder, 30-35 hp cars.

The route took the competitors through Belfort to Bregenz, up 6000 feet through the clouds cloaking the Arlberg Pass, and on to Salzburg and Vienna. An incident-packed race finished with Marcel astonishing the spectators at Vienna (It's a *Frenchman*?) who expected the winner to be a Mercedes, by forcing his way through the crowds – insisting that he was not a gate-crasher – and announcing to officials that he had come from Paris! His average speed over the muddy, rutted roads and perilous passes of Europe was 39 mph and his win was achieved in the face of rival cars of up to 60 hp.

The following year, the last and most tragic of the inter-capital contests was run between Paris and Madrid, when Marcel Renault, part-blinded by the dust of another car, took a bend too fast, crashed, and died within hours.

The Paris-Madrid Race of 1903. Louis Renault learns of Marcel's death on the road from his brother, Fernand

Louis Renault gave up racing, concentrating on building his automobile empire. He built cars developed from his racing models – and cars for more prosaic purposes – cabs powered by 2 cylinder 8 hp units, a popular 10 hp model, a 4 cylinder 14 hp based on Paris-Vienna car. In 1906 Renault made their first bus, then 2, 3 and 5 ton trucks, a Grand Prix car of 90 hp (it won the first French Grand Prix, held at Le Mans).

In 1909 'La Société Louis Renault' was formed. Three years earlier Louis had been made a Chevalier de la Légion d'Honneur at the age of 29. 'Boldness of design, independence of spirit, the knowledge of his time . . . and the prodigious capacity for work which animated him, made of this pioneer the most complete captain of industry of the first half of this century.' From garden shed to captain of industry in ten years. The garden shed is still there at Billancourt if anyone needs inspiration.

Top left *Winston Churchill, in Privy Councillor's dress, is driven to Buckingham Palace in a Renault taxi, 1911*
Above *Queen of the road in the 1920s: a Renault 45, with torpedo body by Scaphandier. Not only elegant but with 17 world records*

Top right *Renault's 1926 all-weather 8·3 hp Cabriolet, with Paris chic of the same year*

The house that Adam built

Adam's five sons were bicycle fans. So were a few million others towards the end of the nineteenth century. High-wheeled penny-farthings were the smart machines then, but Opel took advice from the example of British manufacturers, and began to make 'safety' cycles with equal-diameter wheels. The success of the venture was in no small way due to the boys riding a five-saddler pedal-cycle at meetings – such a crazy machine stamped the name of Opel on many a spectator's boggling imagination.

The house of Adam Opel was already famous. Mechanic Opel's first machine – a sewing machine – had been built in 1862 in his uncle's converted cowshed at Rüsselsheim on Main; just four years later he opened a factory, and within a decade his sewing machine was the most popular on the German market.

Old Adam died in 1895, and the older boys, Carl and Wilhelm, took over. They were products of the age – and soon a motor vehicle clattered its way out of the Rüsselsheim works. A mechanic from Dessau called Lutzmann had shown the brothers what Frau Opel called a 'heap of junk' – and from it they had made the first Opel Patent Motor wagon. The Opel-Lutzmann made its public appearance at Heidelberg as a single-cylinder racing car that 'would do thirty on level ground', but the brothers, mindful of road safety and, no doubt, the prejudices of law officers, detuned the road version down to 12 mph.

The Lutzmann vehicle had been much modified by the time the Opels took it out. A new cylinder-boring machine had been developed, a more durable metal for piston rings had been found. Bits and pieces were lightened and the whole vehicle made more roadworthy.

Second phase was a two-cylinder machine; the Opels wanted cars that could convey two people in comfort. No. 2 was a nice car but somewhat funny-looking, with most of its passengers facing the wrong way. It produced no more than pocket-money profits. In fact the Opel Automobile project was eating up all the sewing machine division's profits – and was still money-hungry.

The Opels looked around – and saw a 9 hp French Darracq at the Paris Show. Elegant for the period and just right for the growing German interest in a light car. They made a deal

Above *The Opel brothers made this, their first car, after seeing Lutzmann, a mechanic from Dessau, demonstrate what their mother called 'a heap of junk'.*

The Opels modified it – and produced the 4 hp Opel Patent Motorwagen. Cost in 1898, 'with air-filled pneumatics' : 2900 marks

Opel-Darracq Double Phaeton of 1905

A racing Opel. Three of the five Opel brothers competed in the infant sport at the beginning of the century. Here Carl-Jorns Opel is seen in the 8 litre car entered in the 1907 Kaiserpreis race

with Darracq and imported chassis from France, building bodies in Rüsselsheim.

Carl and Wilhelm were not mere copyists. Opel-Lutzmanns and Opel-Darracqs were fine for a while, but they wanted something that could be called Opel, period.

At the Hamburg Motor Show of 1902 Opel presented a 10/12 hp from their own drawing board. And very modern it was, with a two-cylinder 1884 cc front engine with mechanically operated inlet and exhaust valves, and gear-wheel transmission. A four-cylinder was presented the next year – and began winning sporting prizes for Opel.

The heady excitements of motor sport success caught the imagination of two Opel brothers, Fritz and Carl, and they became two of the best-known sports drivers of their day. In 1905 Opel cars won a hundred sporting victories – a strong factor in the company becoming the leading German automobile producer of the first decade of the twentieth century.

One of the last vehicles to be made before a devastating fire in 1911 reduced the Rüsselsheim works to rubble was one of Opel's most popular – the 'Püppchen' (Dolly) so named for its dainty appearance. From that date the Opel company abandoned its sewing machine manufacture – even though it was then the largest producer in Europe – and concentrated on automobiles.

Above *Many early manufacturers specialised in what they termed a 'doctor's car'. Doctors and patients had reason to be grateful for the extra mobility an automobile provided. This is Opel's 1909 doctor's buggy*

Left *Carl-Jorns poses with the 'best German Entry Cup' in the Kaiserpreis race*

Opposite page *The 4 hp Opel Patent Motorwagen*

The company, although part of the giant General Motors complex since 1928 – a dark year for world economics – had many successes in the automotive field and set up a number of technical advances during the immediate post World War 1 years. As early as 1913 they were making cars of 260 hp in racing form, with speeds up to 142 mph.

Opel was also the first German company to use conveyor systems in production, a change that led, in 1924, to the birth of first quantity-produced German car, the 'Laubfrosch' (Tree Frog) a little four-cylinder 4/12 hp with pressure lubrication, electric starter, inside gear shift and disc clutch. The market was right for this one

Below Opel's first quantity-produced car, the 1924 'Laubfrosch'. **Bottom** *Rak 2, a successful rocket-car—in 1928! This experimental Opel clocked 120 mph on a short run, blasted by 24 gunpowder rockets behind the driver's seat*

too – and by 1928 the output of 42,771 vehicles was ten times that of four years earlier. However, the European depression forced Opel to join GM.

Opel scored another first in the rocket propulsion field. Opel's Rak 1, the world's first rocket-propelled car, was tested, and on May 23 1928, Rak 2, astonishingly modern in appearance, was shown on the Avus track. At its rear-end were 24 gunpowder rockets operated by a pedal. With Fritz von Opel in the hot seat, Rak 2 thundered down the track at 120 mph, its short stabilising 'wings' keeping it down to ground level. The following year Fritz Opel's first rocket-propelled aircraft took to the sky.

Below *The 2½ litre Opel Kapitän, vintage 1951*
Bottom *Opel 1972. This is the sleek and powerful GT/J, with a 1·9 litre powerpack*

Right *Twelve years after the repeal of the 'Red Flag' Act, Britain's motor industry had caught up with the rest of the automotive world. This is a 4-cylinder, 14 hp Wolseley-Siddeley of 1908*
Below *Frederick Lanchester built cars that were designed as automobiles—not converted carriages—and he built the first successful four-wheeled British car. This is a 1903 model, with the 12 hp twin-cylinder power unit in the middle of the chassis*

*British Daimler, 1905. This is the 'Detachable'
model; hooks in the roof allowed it to be winched off,
converting the car into an open tourer. It houses a
4-cylinder 30 hp motor with chain drive. Daimler
cars have been made in England since 1896*

Giovanni Agnelli of Fiat

It is one of the largest manufacturing concerns of *any kind* in the world. It employs nearly a quarter of a million people. Its share of its national market is around 90 per cent; it has 63 production plants and over 12,000 sales points throughout most of the world.

Fiat's early history reads like the birth of a nation. It began in 1899; by 1903 the company was making commercial vehicles in addition to cars. In 1905 F.I.A.T. (as it was written then) founded a ball-bearing company; and went into ship-building the same year. It has made aero engines since 1908, marine engines since 1910, and complete aircraft and locomotive stock since 1915.

And this vast commercial empire grew from the fact that in Verona in 1892 a young cavalry officer found an old oil engine and tried to use it to generate electricity for his house. *Tenente* Giovanni Agnelli hand-made a carburettor for the engine, coupled it up to a dynamo–and blew-up the entire thing. But his interest had been irrevocably captured.

This was a time of industrial movement in northern Italy. Agnelli, with Count Emanuele di Bricherasio and several other financiers, took over the old Ceirano bicycle works, and in 1899 produced the first F.I.A.T. automobile. A tidy-looking model for the day, if a point-or-two old-fashioned, it had a flat-twin cylinder rear-located 679 cc power unit of 3½ hp, face-to-face seats, a maximum speed of 22 mph, a three-speed box, cone clutch and chain drive. About 20 examples were made.

By 1901 the engine had been moved to the front, and had risen to 8 hp and 1082 cc.

Two years later Agnelli produced a very fine 12 hp model of four cylinders. This was a big year for the company, one in which it began exporting to Britain, France and the United States. Total production for the year was a

continued on page 58

First Fiat, 1899. Aboard the 3½ hp vis-à-vis is one of the Fiat founders, Count Roberto Biscaretti di Ruffia, with his family

54

Princess Maria-Laetitia Bonaparte (left), *in the 12 hp Fiat of 1902*

Fiat Tipo Zero 1912: designed to be made in large numbers

Right *A De Dion-Bouton, Model Q, 1903.*
Count Albert de Dion and Georges Bouton went into
partnership in 1883, making first steam vehicles,
then petrol cars. The single-cylinder petrol engine was
used until 1912, but the advanced De Dion axle-and-
suspension system outlived the company by many years
Below *Peugeot, 1895. Four years after the company*
marketed its first car, (five were sold in 1891) this
vis-à-vis was offered. It had twin-horizontal unit of
8 hp, a three-speed box plus reverse, cone clutch and
chain transmission, and could lope along at 30 km/h
Opposite page *Probably the prettiest car of its*
time, this is the 1892 Peugeot vis-à-vis

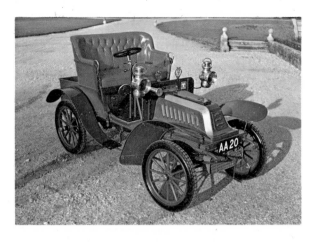

continued from page 54

healthy 134 units. A 12 hp racing car was built, and a 24 hp appeared soon afterwards. By 1903 a 6·4 litre 24-32 hp appeared on Italian roads.

Six months after the plant was opened, a Fiat car scored its initial win in the sport, the first of a long series to come. Fiat's crowning year in motor sport was 1907; the 10·9 litre cars, led by driver Felice Nazzaro, took everything worth racing for – the Kaiserpreis, the Targa Florio and the Grand Prix. Engine sizes were increasing rapidly then and the next year saw Fiat's huge SB4/(Mephistopheles) at England's Brooklands. In 1910–1911, Fiat's big racer was a horrific four-cylinder, 28·3 litre giant, which clocked a hair-raising 132·37 mph during a Belgian test.

Racing in the USA also saw Fiats victorious. The fastest lap of the 1910 national 411-mile race in the United States was made by Nazzaro in a Fiat, and a car of the newly formed Fiat-USA team won in 1911 . . .

The first car-for-the-people from the Fiat works was the Tipo Zero (Model 0) which was offered to the public just before World War I. With the Zero were born two factors which contributed to the immense success of Fiat; large-scale production by flow-line methods, and a cheap, reliable car.

Top *The charming Balilla 508 Sport (Nazzaro at the wheel) in a country setting. First shown in 1933, this 1 litre car with its two-seater bodywork by Ghia had great appeal for the sporting driver of the day*
Above *Fiat of the 1950s: the 1100/103 TV*
Below *1930s: A Fiat 514 Berlina (saloon) bumps down the steps of Urbino cathedral*

58

Herbert Austin

Perfect shelter in bad weather said the advertisement, *Cheap to run, two fine electric lights, businessmen can keep clean; ideal for women because the changing of speed can be done with ease.* That was in 1922, when the first Austin Seven was shown to the British public, the car that, like the Model T Ford, was to put a country on wheels.

In 1922, it was a sharp breakaway from previous motor manufacturing philosophy. The first real mass-made 'baby' car (although Peugeot of France had made its Quadrillette, that was really a cycle-car with, at first, the seats in tandem), the Seven raised some derisive laughter in the year of its birth.

But the 'Chummy', as it became known, was not mere gimmickry. Its 747 cc four-cylinder unit, developing 10 hp at 2400 rpm, could take four people out fishing for the day or climb all but the steepest hills of Cornwall. And it is not all that simple to *walk* up some Cornish hills. In racing form it won many awards.

But the Austin story started much earlier. Born near London, of farming and seafaring stock, Herbert Austin went to school in Yorkshire when the family moved there in 1871. At 16, he was sent off to work for an uncle in

continued on page 62

Herbert Austin, aged 17—just a few months after emigrating to Australia

The first Wolseley automotive product (1895) was a single-cylinder three-wheeler based on a De Dion design, and made by Wolseley's general manager, Herbert Austin

Opposite page *The Vauxhall Iron Works Ltd of London made its first car in 1903. This is the second model, built in 1904, and as a writer in the 'Autocar' of the day said: 'The average cost of running (daily) has worked out one-third that of the upkeep of my horses.' Powered by a water-cooled horizontal motor giving 5 hp, the two-seater version cost 130 guineas*

Below *Straight from the garden shed: Louis Renault's first car, based on a De Dion tricycle, with a 1½ hp engine. Renault used direct drive transmission with a three-speed gearbox on this little voiturette*

continued from page 59

Australia, as were so many other late-Victorian sons. There he learned about sheep, and about machinery that was needed on the farms of the Australian sheep-man. He moved around the country and eventually met, and worked for, Frederick Wolseley. Herbert Austin was asked to return to England to set up a sheep-shearing equipment factory for Wolseley in Birmingham.

There Herbert built his first automobile. In 1895, a tiller-steered three-wheeler, based on a Bollée design, was rolled out of the workshop. A second car was exhibited at London in 1896 — and in 1900 a four-wheeled vehicle powered by a horizontal one-cylinder motor was entered in the Automobile Club of Great Britain's 1000 Mile Trial. It won a silver medal.

Perhaps this award influenced Fred Wolseley, because a year later the Wolseley Tool and Motor Company was formed, with Herbert Austin as manager. Under his direction, Wolseley cars won a high and wide reputation.

By 1905 Austin had resigned after a dispute, and was cycling round the Birmingham region looking for a suitable site for his own factory. He found one, a derelict works at Longbridge just outside the city. He raised cash from several companies, including Dunlop. The Austin Motor Company was in business.

The first car was tried out in April, 1906. It was a moment of some tension. The owner primed the engine, coaxed it, threatened it, wound it. Finally it erupted into smoky life, enveloping Austin and the watchers. Too much oil had been poured in to prevent a possible seizure. When petrol leaks began to be observed, the fuming Austin fired the men responsible for the parts concerned.

However, this first Austin motor car reached the nearby road in one piece, made a successful trial run, and the metal workers were invited to rejoin the Austin company. They did.

The four-cylinder tourer quickly established its reputation for reliability in its first year. With it, Austin had produced a British model that could be called a fully-fledged car—not an adapted carriage.

This initial success encouraged Austin to diversify. His company began to hammer out models of several different styles and shapes, and by 1908 no fewer than 17 were listed.

Below *The 1902 Wolseley 10 hp model, housing a 2-cylinder 2605 cc engine*

Top *The* 1908 *Austin Grand Prix racer, Jack Johnson at the wheel*

Above *The first small Austin–a* 1909 *single cylinder 7 hp tourer*

Right *Fiat (this was the first car to use the abbreviation for 'Fabbrica Italiana Automobili Torino') 12 hp, 1903. Introduced in 1901, it was the first Fiat to house a 4-cylinder unit, the first to be built in series—and the first to be exported*

Below *After an absence of 13 years the most famous of all Austins, the Seven, reappeared in 1952 as the A30. This was the newly-formed BMC's first unitary-construction car*

That year Herbert went into *le sport*, with three special 100-horsepower racing cars entered for the French Grand Prix, and by the following year his cars had become so popular that he had to begin a night shift. His vehicles ranged from 7 to 50 hp and from a single-cylinder car to luxury sizes. Like Fiat in Italy, Austin now spread his manufacture to other fields—industrial and marine engines, commercial vehicles and other allied interests.

But if Herbert Austin had made only a single model, his name would still be recorded as one of the trendsetters of motoring history. His Seven hit the mark so well that motoring took a fast numerical leap forward in Britain.

It was his own design, and Herbert Austin nurtured it as if it were his own kin. He listened to criticism—and made the necessary changes if he thought the complaint was reasonable.

For instance, a customer wrote in 1922 'I am naturally interested in the new seven horse power . . . but disappointed to note that he [Austin] has not fitted running boards . . .' A short time later there appears in the company records 'July: Wings and running boards fitted from A.1–960 Series Three.'

It was offered at Olympia in 1922 at £225, and would-be motorists who had previously had to pocket their dreams of a car, now had a genuine opportunity of buying one. The motoring

Above *The famous Austin Seven, born 1922– the car that, like the Model T Ford in the United States, put Britain on wheels. The price in 1922 was just £225, a sum of money that the man-in-the-street could afford*

Below *Austin traditional. A town carriage with a 4-cylinder 15 hp power unit and an air of bygone days–even for 1911*

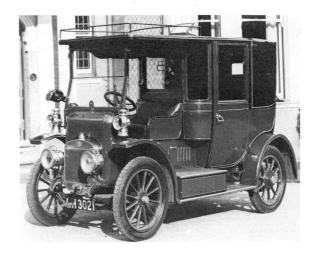

journals were enthusiastic and the public responded.

Through the 17 years of its life, the Seven was constantly modified, entering its maturity with foot-operated four-wheel brakes (previously operated in twos by foot and handbrake) in 1930.

Herbert Austin, farmer's boy from Little Missenden, often called 'the father of the British motor industry', was created a Baron in 1936, when he took the title of Lord Austin of Longbridge. He died in 1941.

Austins were popular on the racing circuit in Britain during the 1930s, and the Seven achieved its share of successes, holding, at one time, all the records for its class. **Below** *An Austin Seven Special (with twin overhead camshafts) circulates at Donnington Park in 1938*
Plenty of action for the Mini. In the 1960s and 1970s, countless international events were won by the little front-wheel-drive car, including the Monte Carlo Rally. **Bottom** *We see rally champion Paddy Hopkirk bouncing over a mountain-top*

To switch on or to stoke up?

Care for a ride in a Stanley steamer? It won't take more than about 20 minutes to steam up and get under way.

First we build up the fuel pressure by working this lever on the floor. It is rather like pumping up a spirit stove when camping, and pumps air into a small fuel tank which primes the burner and supplies the pilot light.

Now we take this piece of hose connected to a small acetylene tank lying in the tool kit. Open a valve on the tank, light a nozzle on the end of the hose and play the flame over the pilot jet to get it hot.

We open the pilot valve and light the pilot light, then open the firing-up valve and let the petrol burn for half a minute on the main burner to warm it.

Now we can open the valve to the main fuel tank and soon the paraffin is beginning to heat the water in the big, drum-like boiler under the bonnet. The flames are roaring. We are almost ready to go now.

Keep an eye on the steam pressure gauge. It is nearly at 300 and that's enough to start. Release the handbrake and we are off. No, there's no starter, no clutch, no gears. The throttle lever on the steering column increases the speed-up to 60 mph if you like. To stop we have to close it and use the brake pedal. *Nothing to it really, is there?*

The Age of Steam

Steam was the obvious choice of power for the first cars because of the wide use that was already made of steam engines. But at first, as we have seen in an earlier section, steam engines were mainly used in heavy vehicles.

Amédée Bollée the elder, a Le Mans bell-founder, started with 'L'Obéissante,' a 4½-ton bus big enough to carry a dozen people in 1873; two years later he drove 120 miles to Paris in it.

A smaller vehicle, 'La Mancelle,' followed, which could reach 25 mph on level ground, but it failed to bring in the hundreds of orders for which he had hoped. Bollée returned to buses and coaches, and 'La Nouvelle,' a three-ton bus, ran in the Paris-Bordeaux-Paris race of 1895, coming ninth, the only steamer to finish.

Count Albert de Dion and his partner Georges Bouton made steam cars in France before they began to concentrate on petrol-engined cars,

it was Léon Serpollet, son of a French blacksmith, who made the big breakthrough in steam motoring.

In 1897 he patented a car with a flash boiler, which was a heated metal tube bent into coils like a spiral spring, through which water passed and was vaporised into pressurised steam. Instead of a heavy boiler to store a supply of steam, the flash boiler produced small quantities of virtually instantaneous steam. The system was lighter and more compact.

Before setting out, the driver lit a charcoal fire, then allowed 10 minutes or so for the tube – originally made of iron, then copper – to heat, after which he worked a lever which pumped water into the tube. After this initial filling, the engine-driven pump took over. Speed was controlled by opening or closing a tap which regulated the flow of water. Top speed was about seven mph.

Serpollet's car worked normally at a pressure of 300 lb per square inch, though the boiler would withstand up to five times that pressure. The boiler and firebox were mounted behind the rear axle; the water tank, holding enough water to take the car 12 miles, was beside the two-cylinder engine under the car's single seat. The three-wheeled vehicle had handlebar steering.

At first, Serpollet had to get police permission every time he wanted to take it on the road, but after a while he was given a permanent permit, an early version of the driving licence. In a two-seat model in 1890, Serpollet and a companion travelled 300 miles from Paris to Lyon, though they took 15 days on the journey.

In 1897 he replaced the charcoal or coke fire with a paraffin burner which was much less bother, and by 1900 he could claim among his customers the Prince of Wales (later Britain's King Edward VII). Serpollet went on to build 6-hp and 12-hp models and in 1902, driving a specially streamlined 6-hp car, nicknamed the Easter Egg, on the Promenade des Anglais at Nice, he captured the world land speed record at 75·06 mph.

The twin brothers F. E. and F. O. Stanley were running a photographic plate business in Newton, Massachusetts, when, at the age of 53, F. E saw his first steam car, an import from Europe. He decided he could build a better one – and a year later he had done so. The twins

sold it and built two more. In 1899 they built 200 small, open two-seaters with the engine and boiler beneath the seats.

The boiler was drum-shaped and held about 300 vertical copper fire-tubes, surrounded by water. A petrol burner below sent heated gases up the vertical tubes and eventually out through a smoke-box at the back of the 5-cwt car.

Top speed was about 25 mph and fuel and water gave a range of only 60 miles, but improvements followed rapidly.

In 1906 the twins sent Fred Marriott, their chief mechanic, with a lightweight Stanley Rocket to Florida where he reached 127·56 mph. The following year, with the steam pressure at 1300 lb per square inch – more than double the usual pressure – he was travelling at about 150 mph when the car hit bumps on the sand, hurtled through the air and was smashed to pieces. Marriott was badly hurt and the Stanleys never raced again.

Some said Marriott was travelling at close on 200 mph when he crashed – but this is only a legend, one of scores that surrounded the Stanley. Others claimed that a locomotive engineer's licence was needed to drive a Stanley and that boilers exploded with terrifying results. They were all just legends.

Other makes of steam car achieved popularity. One was the White, which was used by President Theodore Roosevelt on official engagements in 1906, and which was bought in some numbers to provide squad cars for the New York Police Department. It made steam faster than the Stanley but did not have the same reserve of power. Whites ceased production in 1912; in that year the Stanleys reached their peak of production with 650 cars.

In 1918, F.E. ran off a road to avoid two farm carts and was killed. F.O. quit the business, which continued until 1924, when the last Stanley left the factory.

By this time Abner Doble in California had produced the Rolls-Royce of steamers, a car

Opposite page *Léon Serpollet at the wheel of his steam car at the 1901 Cordingley Motor Show*
Below *Twins F. E and F. O. Stanley built their first steam automobile in 1897 at Newton, Mass. Here they are putting it through handling tests*
Right *By 1904, the Stanley brothers had developed a functional and sophisticated vehicle, the 8 hp runabout, which they sold to enthusiastic fire departments in the United States, for $750 each*
Below right *Stanley steam power again, around 1910. Three years earlier, a Stanley had reached 150 mph on a timed run*

which could be driven away from cold in less than a minute. One just turned a key and had 750 lb pressure within seconds, thanks to the use of an electric generator and sparking plug. Like the later Stanleys, the Doble had a condenser to cool used steam for re-use.

Two years later a Doble could cover 750 miles on 30 gallons of water and hit a top speed of 90 mph. But it was ten times the price of the Stanley. Only about 60 were sold. It ceased production around 1932, and steam on the roads was then effectively dead.

Over the years there had been more than 100 different steamer marques, most of them American. At first the steam enthusiasts had sneered at the rival petrol cars. Steam cars were as fast, ran more smoothly and had fewer moving parts. There was nothing to choose in appearance. The new gasoline cars needed heavy quantities of expensive fuel and had difficulty in climbing hills, even with crude gears.

But the victories of petrol cars over steamers in the early motor races began the decline in steamer sales. The public had never really taken to steam on the roads. They distrusted the roaring blue flames and the pilot light (which had to be turned off in garages and on ferries) and they were thoroughly scared by the roar and hiss of surplus steam blown off in traffic hold-ups.

The début of the electric self-starter in petrol-engined cars in 1912 sounded the death knell for the steamer.

Battery Power

At the beginning of the century, Thomas Edison claimed that the nickel-alkali battery he was developing would solve all the problems of electric propulsion for cars and make the steamer and the petrol-engined car redundant. It didn't.

Then, as ever since, batteries have always been the problem factor with electric cars. The first crude electric vehicle was made in Scotland in 1839, but this was before the days of rechargeable batteries, and it had no prospect of becoming

viable. Thirty years later, Gaston Plante's invention of the accumulator or storage battery had changed the situation, but it was still not until 1888 that Fred Kimball of Boston produced the first battery-driven car in America.

In the same year, the first electric bus, designed by Walter Bersey, was seen on the streets of London, to be followed two years later by a regular service. In 1891, William Morrison of Des Moines, Iowa, became the first man to make and sell an electric car.

In 1898 the Riker Motor Vehicle Company of Elizabethport, New Jersey, produced a two-seat three-wheel car, and the Electric Vehicle Co. of Hartford, Connecticut, began making the famous Columbia cars.

In Europe, the following year, the Count de Chasseloup-Laubat established the first world land speed record in a Jeantaud electric car at 39·24 mph, and a duel followed between Chasseloup-Laubat and Camille Jenatzy (who built his own electric cars in Belgium), pushing up the record to 65·79 mph a year later.

Electric record-breaking was to end in 1902 when Walter Baker, crashed in a streamlined car powered by 40-cell batteries, killing two people in a record bid on Staten Island, USA.

Records were established over a kilometre course, but even this distance flattened the cars' batteries at the speeds they achieved. The trouble with electric cars was that one could go fast for a short distance or slowly for a greater distance. But one could not go *far* and *fast*.

And yet by 1900 electric cars were everywhere. The first taxis came to the streets of New York. They were Columbia electrics with batteries weighing the better part of a ton.

Columbia were also making trucks and vans, and a four-seater which provided for a driver, with a footman riding at the rear. The Columbia soon had a drive-shaft when the petrol-engined car was still using chain drive. It had electric lights, powered by the batteries. It had a simple control handle, a forward slot giving five forward speeds, a rear slot giving three reverse speeds, governed by the use of resistors.

Henry and Clem Studebaker began their automobile manufacturing career with an electric car which gave 40 miles to a battery charge. The range was limited but electric cars were simple to operate, making them popular with women who could not, or would not, crank a handle to start a petrol-engined car or fire the boiler of a steamer.

In America, the electric car became primarily a town runabout, a woman's car, chintzy and feminine in upholstery and décor. In Edwardian England, it became a gentleman's carriage, chauffeured by a liveried servant, as decorous as it was silent.

Opposite page *Experimental steam in the USA. After the 'primitives' of Europe had led the way, America became the most fertile soil for the steam cult, and a number of manufacturers built their versions of the best way to travel. Since the turn of the century, 100 different marques have lived and died in America*

Left *Thomas Edison with an early Baker electric. The American inventor thought this new battery would solve the travel-restricting re-charging problems of the electric car. He was wrong, but the motor trade has been tinkering with electrics ever since – still trying to overcome much the same problem*

Below *The Doble steam car was produced from 1914 to 1932, by which time it was a very fine piece of engineering. It could be driven away from cold in 30 seconds and could travel 750 miles to a single charge of water at a top speed of 90 mph. This is a 1932 Series 'E' Doble*

But in 1912, the easy-starting advantage disappeared with the introduction of the self-starter on the petrol-engined car – the same self-starter that killed the steamer.

Makers of electric cars fought hard. The range had increased to 100 miles to a charge at a speed of 12 mph. The simplicity of foot controls was boosted. The makers of New York's Buffalo car advertised. 'The action of walking is so natural you need never give a thought to how it is done, although to start you raise one foot, to stop you place both feet on the ground. Just as simply and unconsciously the owner of a Buffalo Electric controls the starting, stopping and speed of his car, all by the foot control, an exclusive Buffalo Electric feature.'

In fact, the release of the foot pedal released the expanding shoe brakes. The car then started, its speed determined by the distance the pedal was allowed to rise. There was just one pedal to operate, and this feature was soon common to electric cars.

But in the 1920s the electric vehicle virtually died, save for delivery vans where speed was of little importance compared to easy starting and stopping and silence.

However, work continued on the development of both steam and electric cars, and has today gained importance in the drive to free cities from noise and the pollution of the internal combustion engine's fumes.

Future for Steam and Electric Cars?

In steam, the search in recent years has been for a new operating fluid to replace water—for water needs a lot of heating to create steam and, of course, it freezes easily in cold weather. What is needed is a compound with a low freezing point, amenable to being evaporated and condensed repeatedly, non-toxic and fire-resistant. Attention has been turned to the fluids used in refrigerators, one of the most used being Freon, which freezes at minus 168 degrees F. Although it is considerably more expensive than water, the Japanese motor industry has conducted several successful experiments with it.

In the United States, General Motors experimented with a Chevrolet Chevrelle fitted with a Besler steam engine, but it was heavier than the normal Chevrelle V8 and developed only half the power.

The electric car is still, as it has been for the past half-century, the great hope of the future among environmentalists. The problem remains one of speed and range from a battery charge, and one suggestion has been development of a car with dual propulsion, electric for the city streets and internal combustion for the motorway.

The dream persists for a fuel cell in which fuel is converted into electricity without the need for an intermediate engine and gearbox.

Above *Ford prototype electric car, the Comuta. Designed as a future city car to sell (in 1970) at about £700, this little bug will do 35 mph. However, it has the same old catch: with stop-start town conditions it would probably drain its batteries after about 15 miles. Keep trying, Ford!* **Below** *Steam renaissance? The 1969 Chevrolet SE-14, with Besler engine. Packed with expander, combustion chamber, steam generator, condenser, the works may baffle even the expert internal-combustion man. Start-up time is 30 seconds*

A car for the multitudes – Henry Ford

Henry Ford's place in the history of the United States and in the motoring world is familiar to everyone – despite his alleged statement that history is bunk. After putting America on wheels, his vast company was instrumental in bringing personal motor transport to the ordinary man in Britain from 1911, when Ford opened a factory in Manchester. Until 1932, Ford's British production models were right-hand drive versions of American models. In Germany, Ford began assembling the Model T in 1925, and six years later Ford-Werke AG was formed. Ford's French activity lasted from 1947 to 1954, when Simca took over.

From his earliest days in the industry – he made his first vehicle in the shed behind his home in Detroit in 1896 and his first commercially produced car (the Model A) in 1903 – Henry Ford had promised to 'make a car for the multitudes' and that, after one or two essays into more exotic fields, is precisely what he did. Now, very few mature motorists on either side of the Atlantic have not owned a Ford sometime during their driving days. Here in pictures is a brief glimpse of the work of Henry Ford and his successors over the past seventy turbulent automotive years . . .

Henry in his first car, the 1903 Model A

This stripped-down car, 999, brought Henry Ford (seen here with Barney Oldfield at the wheel) a brief world speed record when he drove it at a timed 91·37 mph in 1904

Model T, 1910, with family. Ford moved to a bigger factory at Highland Park, Michigan, in this year

Henry Ford (1863–1947) founded the Ford Motor Company in 1903, with 11 other stockholders. He got 225 shares in exchange for his designs

*The famous Model T was announced early in 1908,
and went into production in October. It was so
successful that Ford was frequently forced to tell*
*dealers to close their order books. When production of
the Model T ceased in 1927, precisely 15,007,033
had been sold*

74

Production line, 1923. Flowline had been introduced as early as 1913, when the cars were put on skids and moved by a tow-rope along the line of parts

Chatting with the girl next door—or admiring her 1926 Coupé?

The Model T reaches maturity: the 1923 sedan

Model Y, reduced to a £100 price in 1935

The 1951 Ford 2-door. Automatic transmission had become available a year previously

Ford at Le Mans, 1964. The GT 40 first appeared in April, with a 4·2 litre power-unit developing 350 bhp at 7200 rpm. The mid-1960s were memorable for the Ford/Ferrari battles on the world's racing circuits

The first races

The world's first real motor race got under way at midday on June 11th, 1895, when, after a procession across the pavé from Paris to the Place d'Armes at Versailles, 22 cars set off on a main road route for Bordeaux and back, a distance of 732 miles.

Competing were 15 petrol-engined cars, six steamers and one electric vehicle.

At first a De Dion steamer took the lead, but it broke down at Vouvray and 53-year-old Emile Levassor forged ahead in his Panhard-Levassor with its 3½ hp 1200 cc Daimler engine.

By 3.30 next morning, he had reached Ruffec, 252 miles from the start line, but he was so far ahead of the estimated time of arrival that his relief driver was still sleeping. Rather than wait and jeopardise the lead he had built up, Levassor carried on, his eyes straining to pierce the darkness. He reached Angoulême at 5.30 am and by 10.40 am he was in Bordeaux, nearly four hours ahead of his nearest rival. He turned, drove through the excited crowds, and set off on the return leg.

At Ruffec, his co-driver was waiting this time, but Levassor was jealous now, not only of his lead

but of the fact that he had achieved it single-handed, so he declined to hand over the tiller and carried on to reach the finish line at 1 pm on June 13th, with an astonishing lead of nearly six hours over the next car, a Peugeot.

He had been at the tiller of the car for 48 hours and 48 minutes. His longest break was 22 minutes. And he had averaged nearly 15 mph. Only eight petrol-engined cars and one steamer finished the race and Levassor's was a feat which has never been surpassed – and never will be for no race organiser today could, or would, permit it.

'Yet he did not appear to be over-tired,' wrote the Marquis de Chasseloup-Laubat afterwards. 'He wrote his signature at the finish with a firm hand. We had lunch together at Gillet's at the Porte Maillot. He was quite calm; he took with relish a cup of bouillon, a couple of poached eggs and two glasses of champagne; but he said that racing at night was dangerous.'

So ended the world's first motor race. It had grown out of the Paris-Rouen Trial a year before for a £200 prize put up by the newspaper 'Le Petit Journal'. M. Griffard, the editor, had been

Opposite page *11 June 1895, and the world's first motor race is about to start from Paris. Emile Levassor at the start-line in his Panhard*

Below *The great Paris-Vienna inter-city race of 1902: competitors arrive at the Belfort checkpoint before running through Switzerland*

in a fury. A crime had been committed in nearby Saint-Denis and his newspaper was due to go to press in an hour. How could he travel out there, get the news, write his report and put his paper to bed on time? He couldn't. But it gave him an idea. His old friend Emile Levassor had a device that could move around at a fair speed, although it usually involved more screw-driving than road-driving. 'Why not encourage these horse-less-carriage engineers to make more reliable motors?' thought M. Griffard. Organise a contest, that was it, a competition that would award a prize to the most reliable self-propelled carriage. That 80-mile run had attracted a mass of entries, including 38 petrol-engined cars, 30 steamers and a dubious collection purporting to be powered by levers, pedals, compressed air and even the weight of passengers. Most of these failed to start.

Although it was officially called a reliability trial, it developed inevitably into a race to be first into Rouen, and this honour went to Count Albert De Dion, driving a De Dion-Bouton steamer, who covered the course at an average of 11·6 mph.

But this vehicle was essentially a tractor rather than an automobile, for the passengers rode in a two-wheel trailer behind the steamer, so the organisers ruled that it failed to comply with the spirit of the competition and divided the first prize between the runners-up, a Peugeot and a Panhard-Levassor which were five minutes behind.

Although the horseless carriage was still so novel that many races were gymkhana-type events in which cars were set to compete against horses and cyclists (not always to the credit of the cars) the popularity of the Paris-Rouen Trial and Paris-Bordeaux-Paris race established inter-city drives from Paris as the pattern for most major events in the years following.

In 1896, the big race was from Paris to Marseilles and back – 1062 miles, in daily stages to avoid perilous night driving. Once again a De Dion steamer took the lead; once again Levassor took over. On the second day there was a storm which blew out the burners of cars with hot tube ignition. Levassor kept going, but between Lyon and Avignon he hit a dog – one of 15 that

Panhard & Levassor 4-seater

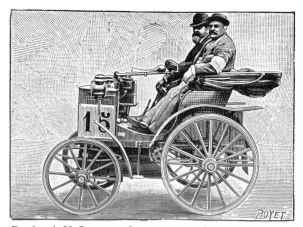
Panhard & Levassor 2-seater

Peugeot frères 3-seater

Peugeot frères 4-seater

were to be killed in the race – and his car turned over. Levassor righted it and drove on, handing over at the half-way mark this time.

He was unplaced, though there was consolation for him in the fact that another Panhard, driven by his works manager, won the race, and other Panhards were second and third. But it was Levassor's last big race. The next year he died, due it is thought, to internal injuries sustained in his crash. Motor racing had claimed its first ace.

The inter-city races went on, with cars growing bigger and more powerful year by year. It required considerable strength even to crank them into life. And keeping them running called for mechanical skill and ingenuity.

Then, in 1903, the inter-city races ended abruptly in disaster. The big race that year was from Paris to Madrid. One hundred thousand people were at Versailles to watch the 250 cars depart at one-minute intervals before dawn on a Sunday morning in May. Millions more were gathering along the route.

The increase in speeds due to the brutish power units favoured by the racers, coupled with the dangerous weakening of the cars by boring holes everywhere they could be bored, in the quest for lightness, had made accidents predictable. With weekend crowds ignoring all warnings and swarming over the roads, and with summer dust stirred into blinding clouds by the speeding cars, so that drivers were steering by glimpses of the tops of telegraph poles, carnage was inevitable, and the event was to become known as 'the race of death'.

One driver smashed into a tree and another into a house. In trying to avoid a child one driver killed a mechanic, a soldier and the child as well. Marcel Renault's car turned over, crushing him to death beneath it.

The death toll is uncertain, though it is believed that a score died before Louis Renault, who had been hitting 90 mph, headed the procession into Bordeaux, 340 miles on. There the French authorities stopped the race. Competitors were not even allowed to drive back to Paris; the cars were ordered on to trains for freighting back. The race was over and the Paris series of races was over for all time. A search began for quiet roads that could be used as circuits. It was the end of motor racing's first era.

Opposite page *First-prize-winners in the first motor race ever run, Paris-Rouen, organized by Le Petit Journal in 1894*

Below *The tragic Paris-Madrid race, 1903. Marcel Renault touching 80 mph, minutes before arriving at the fatal bend at Couhé-Verac where he was killed*

Racing in America

France was the birthplace of motor racing, but the Paris-Rouen Trial had been publicised in America by a diligent reporter working for the 'New York Herald' who accompanied the competitors over the route on a bicycle. And the enthusiasm with which his reports were greeted played a part in the decision of the 'Chicago Times Herald' to organise the country's first real motor race on Thanksgiving Day, 1895.

Six cars slithered through slushy snow on a 54-mile course; the winner was Frank Duryea in a car of his own make, in 8 hours 23 minutes. Only one other car finished, and Duryea had his share of troubles with repairs needed to steering, gearing and ignition. But he had the great advantage of being serviced by his brother Charles, who took short cuts between points on the course in a horse-drawn sleigh loaded with parts. In fact, he provided a mobile workshop – the forerunner of those used by works teams in big rallies today.

Then, in 1904, William K. Vanderbilt organised the first Vanderbilt Cup race on the dirt roads of Long Island, New York. It was full of incident: a Mercedes turned over after a tyre burst, killing the riding mechanic. A Pope-Toledo lost its steering and hit a tree. George Heath was first to finish the 284·4-mile course in 6 hours 56 minutes, driving a 90 hp Panhard, and Albert Clement was second in an 80 hp Clement-Bayard.

But the race was stopped before the third man arrived because the crowds were as enthusiastic and undisciplined as those of France, and had swarmed across the road.

Nevertheless, the Vanderbilt races continued until 1910, when four deaths and a score of injuries among drivers and spectators caused them, like the Paris races, to be moved to the country.

Over to the Track

In Europe, the search for ways of continuing motor racing in urban areas resulted in Hugh Locke-King, a rich British businessman, spending a quarter of a million pounds in 1907 to build the world's first permanent racing circuit on land he owned near Weybridge, Surrey. Its name was Brooklands.

Even before the official opening, Selwyn Edge, of Napier Cars, was roaring round the three-mile long banked concrete track in an attack on the world 24-hours record which then stood at 1096 miles. Edge intended not only to beat this figure but to motor at over 60 mph for the entire 24 hours.

His car was a green $7\frac{3}{4}$ litre Sixty Napier, and he had two others—one white and one red—to pace him. The attempt began at six in the evening so that he could complete the night driving while fresh. Three hundred lanterns placed around the circuit aided the acetylene lamps of the Napier.

In his first hour he put in 70 miles. In the remaining hours, despite rain which drenched him, despite a stone which smashed his windscreen, he never did less than 61 miles in the hour, and in his best hour he did 72. He finished the 24-hours with 1581 miles completed at an average of 65·9 mph.

The track then opened, and the first race (won by a Napier entered by Edge and driven by Hugh Tryon) was the Marcel Renault Memorial Plate. Motor racing in the early days of Brooklands took much of its terminology from horse racing and drivers wore coloured smocks like those of jockeys, for recognition.

During the second Brooklands Season, 1908, Edge issued challenges on behalf of Napier for stakes ranging from £1000 to £10,000. The most publicised was a duel with Felice Nazzaro in Mephistopheles, an 18-litre Fiat. Edge put up Ernest Newton in the biggest Napier, a 90 hp Six of over 20 litres named Samson.

After every outfitters in Weybridge had been visited, because Nazzaro had lost his black driving gloves and would not start without an identical pair, the race got under way. The Napier led for the first three of the six laps but then a crankshaft failed and the Fiat SB4 had no more competition.

They were halcyon days at Brooklands before the first World War. For a few shillings any enthusiast could try his skill on the banking on non-race days. World speed records were set there. Motor manufacturers took advantage of the high-speed opportunities to test their products and learn lessons about the durability of components. The value of the permanent race track was established.

In America, Carl Fisher, bicycle racer turned barnstorming motor dealer, created the Indianapolis circuit in 1909. Two years later came the first Indianapolis 500 mile race, which was won by Ray Harroun, who came out of retirement as a Marmon works driver to take the wheel of a yellow and black Marmon Wasp.

He was the only driver in the race who was not accompanied by a riding mechanic and he won by ignoring the pace-setting competitors and holding as far as he could to a consistent 75 mph to cut down changes of tyres necessitated by the brick surface of the track. He finished in 6 hours 42 minutes at a speed of 74·59 mph.

Birth of the Grand Prix

It was an American who established the first great international motor racing series and thereby, unintentionally, brought about the birth of Grand Prix races. In 1900, James Gordon Bennett, owner of the 'New York Herald', put up a trophy for an annual international race in France. It was open to teams of three cars from national clubs, and the first race—250 miles from Paris to Lyon—was won by the Panhards of France.

Races from Paris to Bordeaux and Paris to Innsbruck followed, but the end of inter-city racing meant the end of the Gordon Bennett series in their original form. They were switched to road circuits, the first being a figure-of-eight circuit in Ireland.

Two years later, however, the Gordon Bennett races died, largely due to French complaints that though they were the world's greatest motoring nation and produced more cars than any other nation they were only permitted the same three-car team as any smaller car-producing country. The French withdrew and in 1906 started the French Grand Prix. The first event—of 770 miles—was staged at Le Mans, though not on the famous circuit of today. It was won at 63 mph by F. Szisz, a Hungarian, in a Renault powered by an engine of nearly 13 litres—and that was by no means the biggest in the race.

In 1907, in an attempt to halt the growth of the monsters, petrol consumption limitations were introduced—with little effect. In 1908 restrictions on bore size were introduced—again with little effect. For three years the Grand Prix lapsed and when it was held again in 1912 the miracle had been worked. Georges Boillot roared to victory in a new Peugeot producing a speed of 100 mph from only 7·6 litres.

In 1913 he won again, with a car of still smaller capacity, and the stage was set for the 1914 Grand Prix, the event in which motor racing came to maturity.

Below *A 1927 Vauxhall 30/98. Developed from a line of racing and record cars, the 30/98 took part in many sporting events, and won 75 motor races and 14 hill-climb events. The designation 30/98 is a mystery; it is neither 30 nor 98 hp, and no other measurement of the car matches the figure*

The first US cross-country race, staged by Oldsmobile in 1905. 'Old Scout' won, covering an average of 1000 miles a day from New York to Portland, Oregon

Racing at Brooklands, England, 1909. A typical start scene as drivers rev-up their engines

An Era Starts – and Finishes

New regulations limited the cars to engines of $4\frac{1}{2}$ litres or less, yet there was the biggest-ever international entry – 13 official teams comprising 37 cars and every one of them of brand new design. There were Mercedes and Sunbeams, Delages, Fiats, Schneiders, Vauxhalls and Opels. But the favourite, naturally, was Boillot in his new Peugeot.

No one outside the Mercedes équipe knew that the Germans were going to introduce a new element into motor racing – team tactics.

The race was 466 miles, 20 laps of the 23·3-mile course at Lyon. At 8 am, outside the specially-built grandstand, the starter flagged away the first pair, an Alda and an Opel. Thirty seconds later he launched the second pair, a

Nagrane and a Vauxhall, and every 30 seconds afterwards another pair, until 12 minutes later all had set off into the dust.

Ten minutes passed and the first lap leader came into view – the blue Peugeot of Boillot. Into the straight he roared, down the hill to Les Sept Chemins, past the pits and stands – a lap time clocked at 21 minutes and 29 seconds. The French crowd cheered exultantly.

But then came the white Mercedes of Max Sailer and the crowd quietened; Sailer had started 90 seconds after Boillot but had covered the lap 18 seconds faster. He was, in fact, leading the race. The third car, a Delage, and the fourth, a Sunbeam, passed almost unnoticed as spectators worked out the significance of the time differentials.

At the end of the second lap Boillot was still ahead on the road but Sailer was still ahead on time. The French hung out 'Go faster' signs to Boillot and he went faster, but the Mercedes still gained. Suddenly Boillot's tyres were in shreds and he had to stop to change them, Sailer was in the lead on the road as well as in time.

Boillot set off in furious pursuit. He drove hard and fast and well, and at the end of lap five he passed Sailer's Mercedes, stopped in the country with a broken crankshaft. Boillot was the leader again and the French rejoiced that all was once again as it should be. What they did not know was that Sailer's job had been done. He had been given the task of harassing Boillot, of making him drive over his limit, and over the limit of safe engine revs. Sailer's car had been deliberately expendable.

The Germans signalled to their second man, stocky Christian Lautenschlager, winner of the 1908 Grand Prix. He moved into second place, ahead of the Mercedes of Wagner and Salzer, and continued to harass the Frenchman. When Lautenschlager had to halt at the pits to refuel, his team mates held their stations, and held off Jules Goux in the second Peugeot and several Delages, until he was back in position.

Boillot gritted his teeth and drove the race of his life. On lap 16 he was two minutes ahead of Lautenschlager. But the effort was taking its toll of his car. At the end of lap 17 there came an ominous noise from the area of his rear axle.

His lead began to drop. It dropped to one minute, to 30 seconds, to 16 seconds. Boillot prayed, as all the French at Lyon prayed, for his car to hold out as he took it flying over the bumps and ruts.

The Mercedes overtook and Boillot could do nothing. Just 12 minutes before the end of the race he came to a grinding halt with the differential in pieces. Mercedes took first, second and third places. Lautenschlager first, Otto Salzer second and Louis Wagner (who was, in fact, French) third.

That race, held as war clouds loomed over France, was the most internationally representative ever held up to that point; it also featured the most sophisticated machinery.

Within months war came to Europe and motor racing ended (except in America, where it was to enjoy another three years of life). Brooklands was offered to the country by Locke-King and the Royal Flying Corps took it over. Drivers joined the Armed Forces and an early casualty was Georges Boillot, suffering a final defeat at the hands of Germany when, as a French fighter pilot, he was shot down over the trenches by a team of three German aircraft.

When peace came and motor racing eventually recommenced it was changed. New regulations carried on the trend towards smaller-engined lighter cars. The age of monsters was over. Cars were more sophisticated and the multi-cylinder engines and superchargers became commonplace. New names like Bugatti and Alfa-Romeo replaced those of Panhard and Mors.

In many ways a golden age of motor racing and record breaking was beginning. But the days of the pioneer sportsmen, the days when every driver *had* to be a hero, were over.

The French Grand Prix, 1914: a Mercedes victory by team tactics. The 466-mile event was won by Christian Lautenschlager (No. 28) with team mates Salzer and Wagner second and third

Motor sport now: 1

It began in a paraffin-lit café on the Place Pigalle in Paris, where the editor of 'Le Petit Journal' put up the idea of a Paris to Rouen rally in 1894. That famous 'first' soon triggered off another sporting event the following year, and a dozen others with a couple of seasons.

Motor sport soon became a lusty infant and, only six years into the twentieth century, the first Grand Prix had been run.

Today, the sport is a powerful giant on which millions are spent every year – and which reaps millions through its strength as a selling weapon for tyres, fuel, oil, parts and, of course, in many cases the cars themselves. Here are some of today's racing vehicles, including one or two of the immediate past, a comparison that will indicate that the developments in automobile engineering are by no means decelerating.

Top *Graham Hill, born 1929. World Champion in 1962 and 1968. Winner of the Indianapolis 500 in 1966, and victor of more than 18 Grands Prix*
Above *Small-formula racing in France*
Left *Formula 5000, a Surtees-Chevrolet TS II, 1972*

Formula 1 racing in the 1970s. A March 701
driven by Sweden's Ronnie Peterson leads a pack
around Druid's Bend, a long hairpin at Britain's

2·65 mile Brands Hatch Circuit, where most of the
country's important racing battles are fought

The start of a major Grand Prix at Brands Hatch,
Kent

The sell

As soon as the automobile was commercially produced it had to be advertised. The number of self-propelled vehicles on the roads was not sufficient to be self-proclaiming and the little snippets in the newspapers informing readers about 'the curious horseless carriage propelled by an unknown power seen frightening horses in the high street yesterday' were not the best way of presenting the new motor age to the public.

At first, advertisements simply told people that the automobile company was in business and that they could buy the vehicle today. Some of the early artwork was elegant, tasteful and compelling. But other offerings were dreary, or vainglorious, or melodramatic, or just plain lies. Here are some of the ways in which early advertising departments and PR men tried to make grandfather part with his cash in the hope that he could forget for ever that worst of all chores, mucking out the stable—and some that father saw on the hoardings and in the motoring magazines a generation later . . .

Above *A Lux advertisement of 1901*
Left *Daimler of Germany branches out into commercial vehicles. Advertised is the first Daimler belt-driven farm truck of 1896, with rustic doggerel (translation below)*

A "Daimler" is a handy beast,
it draws like an ox—you can see it here;
it doesn't eat when in the stall,
and *only drinks when work's being done;*
it also does your *threshing, sawing and pumping*
when money's short, as often happens;
it can't catch foot-and-mouth disease
and plays no wicked tricks on you.
It won't toss you on its horn in anger,
nor eat up your precious corn.
So buy yourself a beast like this
and be equipped for good and all.'

The first Fiat advertisement, showing the 3½ hp carriage of 1899

AUTOMOBILES

RENAULT

A 1913 Renault advertisement

This Opel advertisement of 1904 is a fine specimen of commercial art graphics of the period

Peugeot appealed to fashionable Paris with their 1899 2-cylinder phaeton

Controversial Fiat poster, 1934: the Vatican demanded a ban on it until the lady's skirt was draped more properly over the left hip!

Confident Edwardian name-dropping—by Napier

Pampering madame by Citroën in the mid-1920s

The new Dodge Eight five-passenger coupé, as shown in 1931. The familiar Dodge Ram hood ornament first appeared this year

A message without words: modern Pirelli

Veteran
Edwardian
Vintage

The really old ones rally gently from point to point; the Edwardians, ramrod straight with dignity, motor about with very proper decorum; the youngsters of the Vintage period race each other with élan and surprisingly rapid lap-times. From Rolls Royce to Austin Seven they yield a great dividend of pleasure, not only to their owners, but to all who see them, on their colourful days out-of-doors.

Above *Vintage at rest. A 1931 2665 cc supercharged Alfa Romeo*
Top right *Delage at speed on the annual Richard Seaman Trophies Meeting at Oulton Park, Cheshire, England. This is a 1922 5228 cc car specially built by the factory for sprints*
Right *Wheels, levers, handles, horns, mirrors, lights—polished with pride for the day out*

Opposite page, top left *A profusion of plaques for a vintage steam vehicle*
Top right *A 1904 Renault Park Phaeton. It has a special body built by Rothschild of Paris, and won first prize at the 1904 Motor Show*
Below *Edwardian dignity . . . the stark, upright design of the Rolls-Royce frontal area*

Wars on wheels

In 1899, Major R. P. Davidson of Illinois, an instructor at the North West Military Academy, bought a three-cylinder, 6 hp engined Duryea tricar and fitted a swivelling Colt 7 mm, 480-rounds-per-minute machine gun over the front wheel. There was still enough room in the car to carry a crew of four with their tents and 5000 rounds of ammunition for the gun. The major had created a potentially terrible mobile weapon.

It was not surprising. Man has a wayward genius for turning almost any invention to use in waging war and, after all, when Cugnot had designed his steam tractor—the first-ever motor vehicle—back in the eighteenth century, he had intended it for pulling cannon.

In 1900, Davidson up-dated his fighting vehicle by transferring the gun to a four-wheel Duryea. The US Army Chief of Staff, General Nelson Miles, was impressed, and recommended to the Secretary of State for War that five cavalry regiments should be equipped with the cars. But nothing happened.

In 1910, Davidson acquired two Cadillacs and fitted each with two skyward-pointing machine guns for fighting balloons and airships. In France, a Captain Genty had by this time put guns on a Panhard and in England F. R. Simms had fitted one to a De Dion-Bouton.

But senior military minds were more interested in the automobile in its basic role as a personnel carrier. In Britain, the then young and brash Automobile Association conceived the idea of moving a whole battalion of troops into battle by a fleet of motors. They put forward a scheme to test the idea in 1909, promising to get some 300 of their members with their cars and trucks on to the streets.

The War Office was sufficiently alert to the possibilities to provide 1000 Grenadier, Coldstream and Scots Guards, and the AA undertook to move them 63 miles from London to Hastings.

The biggest problem was the transportation of the men's machine guns, ammunition, stretchers, entrenching tools and cooking equipment. Motorists were not ready to risk damaging their vehicles by shifting those, but a London taxicab company owner came to the rescue, taking 30 cabs off the streets, removing their bodies and replacing them with platforms on which the loads could be lashed.

On the morning of March 17, the Guards stepped into their cars with their packs and rifles at three embarkation points in London and three columns of automobiles moved off to converge into one at the Crystal Palace in South London.

The manoeuvre was a brilliant success. Its immediate effect was to bring about the introduction of the chinstrap to military headgear, as the Guardsmen had found it impossible to keep their caps on in the moving cars! The long-term effect was more militarily significant—contributing to the promotion, both in Britain and in Germany, of Motor Volunteer Reserves, pools of drivers who would offer their vehicles and their services in the event of war.

Wednesday, March 17th, 1909.
(St. PATRICK'S DAY)

A BATTALION
OF HIS MAJESTY'S GUARDS
WITH TRANSPORT

Will pass along the **Hastings Road TO-DAY**

returning to London in the afternoon.

IT IS BEING CONVEYED IN SEVERAL HUNDRED

MOTOR CARS.

Will all Drivers, Cyclists, & Pedestrians
Kindly keep as closely as possible to the near side of the road as the Cars go by.

THE AUTOMOBILE ASSOCIATION,
PRINCES BUILDINGS,
COVENTRY STREET,
LONDON, W.

This notice was posted on the route of an experimental British troop transport in 1909

Motors for the Services

The conflict came. On August 3, 1914, Germany declared war on France and the next day Britain declared war on Germany. On the following day the appeal went out for motors for the services. Thousands were offered. Most were used for general transport and ambulances but bigger cars, like the stately Rolls-Royce, were given primitive armour plating to become armoured fighting vehicles.

Buses and taxis were commandeered to transport British troops to the front lines of France. Suddenly, almost overnight, the age of the horse was past.

On Friday, July 31, 1914, the British Daimler works in Coventry had closed for the annual staff holidays, so when war was declared the employees were at the seaside. His Majesty's War Department did not wait. Officers descended on the factory and commandeered every motor and commercial vehicle on the premises, quickly stencilling them with the letters 'WD'.

When the Daimler employees returned, their numbers were soon increased from 4000 to 6000 and they were put to work turning out military staff cars, trucks and ambulances.

Foster tractors fitted with 105 hp Daimler engines were adapted for heavy transport tasks, including the towing of 15-inch howitzers, and these tractor-limbers with their 8-foot diameter rear wheels were so successful cross-country that they inspired the birth of the tank.

The first tank, 'Little Willie,' used the same 105 hp engine and the gearbox and differential from the tractor; its debut at the Somme in 1916 is history.

Vauxhall at Luton, a few miles north of London, had just built their first dozen of the 30/98, which was to become one of the most successful sports cars of all time, when war broke out. Its success had to wait until the 'twenties. The Vauxhall staff were switched to building nearly 2000 D-type staff cars.

These 25 hp staff cars (all open, except for a few closed models for the exclusive use of generals and above) served all over the areas of conflict. One carried General Allenby on his victorious entry into Jerusalem in 1917. One carried King George V across the mud of Flanders to Vimy Ridge. One made two crossings of the Greek and Albanian mountain ranges between Salonika and Santa Quaranta on the Adriatic. Another was the first car to cross the Rhine into Germany after the 1918 armistice.

Yet probably the most-used car in the war was the Model T Ford. The British alone had 19,000 of them. At first they were used as

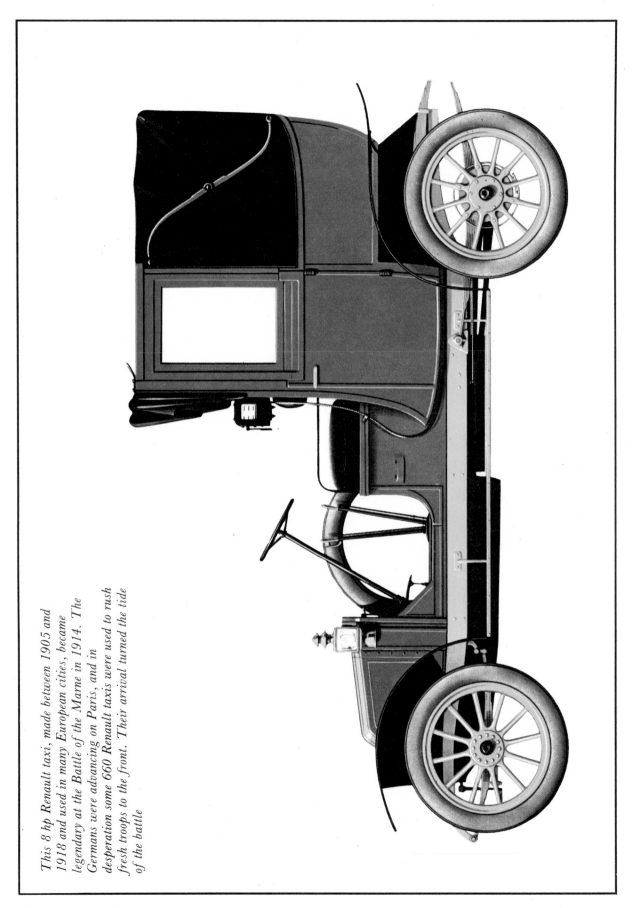

This 8 hp Renault taxi, made between 1905 and 1918 and used in many European cities, became legendary at the Battle of the Marne in 1914. The Germans were advancing on Paris, and in desperation some 660 Renault taxis were used to rush fresh troops to the front. Their arrival turned the tide of the battle

ambulances, but later as light patrol cars, raiding far behind enemy lines and far from service depots, in the Near Eastern desert. In Palestine, Lawrence of Arabia's force used six of them equipped with Lewis guns–and the ideas of Davidson and Genty and Simms came to fruition. Model T's with flanged wheels were also used like trains, on rails, at the Western Front.

By the time the United States came into the conflict in 1917, they had had the benefit of having watched the war for three years. They avoided the use of horses altogether and decided to mass-produce standardised trucks. The same specifications were given to all the major automobile companies, and Packard and Riker and Pierce-Arrow turned out a standard vehicle, known as the Liberty trucks, the most common of which was the 3½ ton model. By the time of the armistice, America had more than 60,000 military vehicles, many of which remained in service until World War 2.

London buses, too, were pressed into military service in World War 1. Here British troops in France board some that will take then back for a rest in 1917

In World War 1, the Ford Model T was one of the mainstays of the British Army. Here one leaves British lines in Syria to demand the surrender of Aleppo, 1918

Above *Staff cars loaded with troops mix with refugees near Péronne during the Somme retreat*
Below *General Allenby rides in victory–transport by courtesy of Vauxhall*

World War 2

The land operations of the Second World War were to be fought almost entirely on wheels and tracks.

In Britain, the start of the war brought an immediate black-out to the streets, and drivers might use their headlamps at night only with approved masks on them, permitting narrow slits of light to escape. This was one of the reasons for the reduction of the speed limit in built-up areas to 20 mph.

Petrol rationing was introduced to the public three weeks after the start of the war and a month's civilian ration could be used up all too easily in one day. Then, in 1942, petrol for pleasure-motoring was banned completely. Gas companies tried to promote gas as an alternative fuel and some cars sprouted roof-top gas-bags for it, but the idea lacked efficiency.

Once again the motor manufacturers were required to turn over to war production, making aircraft and aircraft engines, steel helmets and jerricans, tanks and lifeboat engines as well as motors. An early air raid in 1940 on the Vauxhall factory at Luton killed 39, seriously injured 40 and did heavy damage, but the plant was producing vehicles again within a week, and the company built 250,000 Bedford trucks for the services, in addition to Churchill tanks and official cars.

The Daimler company made more than 6500 four-wheel-drive scout cars and 2500 disc-braked armoured cars for use by reconnaissance troops, apart from staff cars used by top British officials when Germany was occupied – despite being plastered by more than 170 bombs during the war.

Austin made more than 120,000 military vehicles, from an 8 hp utility tourer to three-ton trucks, and did pioneer work on the water-proofing of vehicles for seaborne landings.

Jeeps and Bucket Cars

The best-known vehicle of World War 2 was

Petrol was scarce in 1940. Some cars sprouted roof-top gas-bags, but most owners just put their cars in the garage 'for the duration'

undoubtedly the American Jeep, the all-purpose, go-anywhere ¼-ton truck which got its name from the designation GP ('general purpose').

The Willys and Ford prototypes were completed in 1940 and the first production vehicle was on the road in 1941, to be followed by more than 639,000 others. The basic vehicle had a 54 bhp four-cylinder engine with six forward and two reverse speeds, and was 11 feet long.

But the Jeep appeared in many guises. It was first used as a front-line ambulance, but there were some very warlike, heavily armed versions which were used by Britain's Special Air Service. There were flanged-wheel versions for use on railways, gun-towing versions, amphibious types and crane-carriers.

The German equivalent was the Kübelwagen or bucket car. Back in 1933 Hitler had detailed Dr. Ferdinand Porsche to produce a 'people's car'. He had designed the Volkswagen with its rear-mounted 996 cc air-cooled engine, but

before the VW could get into production Hitler was calling for a military all-purpose truck, and so Porsche produced the Kübelwagen, based on his designs for the VW.

The first bucket cars were delivered in 1940 and were largely regarded as ugly and underpowered, though this was rectified by substituting a 1131 cc engine. Then Rommel ordered the car for the Afrika Korps to use in the desert and by the end of the war some 60,000 had been built.

The Kübelwagen was a foot longer than the Jeep but it also spawned many versions. There was the five-geared *Kommandeurwagen* or command car and the smaller *Schwimmwagen* or amphibian. Some of Porsche's creations were also given flanged wheels for rail operation; others had caterpillar tracks. And as the Jeep led to post-war vehicles like Britain's Land-Rover, the Kübelwagen led to the German export success, the VW 'Beetle'.

German war-time Kübelwagen

Used as ambulance, staff car, railway car, armoured vehicle, the Jeep was the best-known product of World War 2. Seated is General Montgomery

Back to basics–and Major Davidson of Illinois, who seemed to be the first to mount a gun on a car. A Bedford carrying an anti-aircraft weapon, circa 1942

99

Rolls and Royce

The story of Rolls-Royce perfection has been told many times—those almost incredible reports of matched walnut fascias and a spare baulk of the same grain held in stock in case the owner scratches the first one, the hand-soldered radiator shells, the meticulous inspection of parts and testing of engines—those stories are now part of the folk-lore of the industry—and most of them are true.

The first Royce car, made by miller's son

Top left *The Hon. C. S. Rolls, son of Lord Llangattock, aviator, co-founder of Rolls-Royce*
Above *The factory at Cook Street, Manchester, in 1904*

Top right *Henry Royce, electrical engineer, son of a miller living in Lincolnshire, 41 years old when he made his first car*

Henry, was an effort to move away from the blacksmith approach to auto building. The car proved silent and reliable and attracted the attention of the Hon. C. S. Rolls, then selling Panhard cars. In 1906, they went into partnership, producing cars of superb quality for clients with money to spare for 'only the best'. Over the years, this inevitably came to mean clients full of age and dignity, and the Rolls-Royce of the past fitted this image.

Recently, however, the company has been changing its own approach to sales through livelier advertising and design modifications to appeal to younger people. So the Shadow offered, when it was first presented to the public in 1965, a new monocoque body, all-independent suspension, automatic height control, disc brakes (they had kept to drums for years), steering refinements and so on, right down to

The Rolls-Royce name was first used at Christmas 1904, in a working agreement between the two men. This is the 10 hp 2-cylinder Rolls-Royce, the first to go into series production

the solenoid-controlled petrol cap. Now, with the sophisticated Corniche, Rolls-Royce appeal is even more universal.

Here in pictures are some of the outstanding –and unusual–models made by the partnership of Rolls and Royce, models that since 1904 have astonished the press and public by their near-perfection.

Above *The famous 40/50 hp Rolls-Royce Silver Ghost was first shown at the Motor Show in London in 1906. The name was suggested by the aluminium-painted body and silver-plated metalwork. The original price (in chassis form) was £985*
Right *Rolls-Royce made Silver Ghosts, then Phantom Is, in Springfield, Massachusetts, from 1920 to 1931. Shown is a 1927 Phantom I*

Top *A 1930 Phantom II Sedanca de Ville, last word in elegance. With a top speed of over 80 mph, it also had remarkable docility.* **Above** *The 1970s: Rolls-Royce produce the superb Corniche, with its smooth and silent 6750 cc power unit, to sell for over £12,500.* **Right** *An image of opulence*

American empire-building

Four stages of time punctuate the progress of motoring in the United States, from the tentative experimental beginnings of the automobile at the end of the last century to the present day.

At first the fact that the spindly, spidery, buggy-like motor car could take two or three persons from point A to point B maybe 30 miles away just a little faster than the horse was so novel that all other considerations of reliability and possible hazards paled before the glorious new pleasure of mobility. Dust, mud and roads like the surface of the moon were taken in happy stride by early travellers, who saw that the automobile put a larger chunk of the world at their feet for the first time in history.

Then, the second stage, lasting until around 1925 just before Ford Model T production ceased. Motor travellers were still in the honeymoon period—and by about 1910 a lot more people had bought at least *something* mechanical on four wheels.

Post-World War 1 authorities had noticed that motoring was here to stay. Some bridges were built; sign-posts, previously belonging to the stage-coach era, began to cater for the faster-moving motorist. Roads—just a few of the more major highways at first—were metalled with the automobile in mind, although automobile de-velopment and production continually out-stripped road improvement, then as it does now. The Model T, slowly and painfully becoming more sophisticated as the years went by, kept a good proportion of Americans on the road, its big road-wheels and high clearance allowing the road-builders just a little more time to lean on their shovels.

This was followed by the stage of more rapid highway development, of careful and urgent study of the motor car and its effect on the environment, its relationship with other trans-port developments, coupled with the decline of the railroads. During this period, which ended with the commencement of World War 2, the United States came to the forefront in the automotive industry, in production figures and innovation if not in engineering quality, and its road system was, in parts of the country, undoubtedly the finest in the world.

Now, in the fourth, and as yet unfinished, period of the story of the US automobile, the country has turned its energies to safety (mainly preventive safety in the design of roads in all their complexities, and the design, and enforce-ment of safety precautions in the construction of vehicles) and to the effect of the automobile on the environment.

The spidery, buggy-like cars of turn-of-the-century America: the first Oldsmobile (1897), practically noiseless and impossible to explode

Dust, mud, and surfaces like the moon's were taken in happy stride . . .

The automobile is number one priority on the American personal domestic budget. To many, if not most, life without personal transport would be unthinkable, and today legislators are forced to curb the freedom of the motorist more severely than ever before. The menace has long been apparent. Now only the most hard-headed thinking and ruthless legislation will maintain the automobile in its role of servant . . .

In the Beginning . . .

. . . were the Duryea brothers, Frank and Charles. In 1892, when it was still a lot easier to sail round the land-mass of America than travel over it, a number of inventive people were working on gasoline engines, although none had yet installed one in a buggy and made it run.

The brothers Duryea, bicycle engineers, built a one-cylinder engine and bolted it into a high-wheeled buggy. It worked and, in 1893, the first internal-combustion-engined car was driven through the streets of Springfield, Mass. Next year they built a two-cylinder model with pneumatic tyres, spark ignition and an atomising carburettor – and in it, the following year, they won the 'Chicago Times-Herald' race, the first motor sport competition in the United States.

This list of Duryea 'firsts' continues with, in 1896, opening the American home-produced market with the manufacture of 13 cars, and the export market by selling one to Britain.

Enter Elwood Haynes (first car, 1894), Charles King (first car, 1896), Ransom Eli Olds (1896), Alex Winton (1896) and the great Henry Ford.

The Paris-Rouen Trial of 1894 in France had given the infant motor industry such a lift that probably up to a couple of thousand young American engineers were busy in the backyard, putting together tortured pieces of metal and rubber in the hope of producing an automobile. The early US races, and the first track race of 1896, fanned the enthusiasm. This multitude of the late-nineteenth-century pioneers had no solid reason to believe that transport was going the way of the gasoline engine (and indeed a large number were concentrating on steam or electricity) but the easier handling and smaller size of the engine drove them and others in Europe along the internal-combustion route. Many, even today, believe them to have been wrong.

However, such was the incentive to make (and sell) a car that before the end of the century there were no less than 45 registered automobile companies in the United States from the grandiosely titled 'Autocar Company of America,' to the 'Woods Motor Vehicle Company' of Chicago. Hundreds more were to be registered in the years immediately following (over 2900 makes have been listed to the present day).

. . . by early travellers, who saw that the automobile put a larger chunk of the world at their feet. A wet chunk, sometimes

Changing a wheel wasn't often as easy as these ladies make it look, circa 1909

The Founders

In Lancing, Michigan, *Ransom Eli Olds* was active in the auto field. He found a backer, formed a company and began designing. Some of his first designs were too expensive, too elaborate, too impracticable–but one, a buggy which was to retail at $650, seemed just right for the home market. The other experimental plans and cars vanished in a factory blaze in 1901; the one-cylinder buggy, happily, survived. From that one model Olds built up his business by developing the famous Curved-Dash Olds-mobile, now one of the classic examples of early American motor manufacture. To R. E. Olds goes the credit of being the first to make cars for the mass-market in the USA, foresight based on the awareness of the different requirements of America from those of Europe, where the car was then a luxury only for the rich. Olds saw that in the United States it could–and would–be used to overcome the lack of communications which were relieved only in part by the railroads.

David Dunbar Buick was born in Scotland, taken to Detroit by his parents, orphaned at five, and a prosperous owner of a marine engine company by his mid-forties, in 1902. Fascinated by the emergent automotive industry, he and two of his engineers came up with a new idea for increasing the efficiency of the gasoline motor. They put the valves in the head and called it

(later) the overhead valve engine or ohv. Buick produced this two-cylinder 22 hp motor in small quantities (six to be precise) in 1903. He made 37 of his Model B in 1904 and 750 the next year– when the firm was bought by *Billy Durant*, to whom it owed its survival. Within a year production rose to 1400.

Meanwhile Durant was forming the General Motors Corporation and in 1908 Buick became one of the first members of the powerful combine. Despite several reverses, the company prospered and even in the worst years of the depression was producing around a quarter of a million cars annually. David Buick had left in 1906, and died in poverty; he had tremendous faith in his first mid-engined car with its advanced overhead valves, and the countless vehicles which bear his name today amply justify his faith.

Automobiles were oddities and auto factories little more than workshops when Cadillac developed the Model A in 1902. From its parent, the machine tool company of Leland, Faulconer and Norton it brought to car-making an intimate knowledge of precision engineering and high quality workmanship.

Henry M. Leland, mainspring of his company, entered the industry when Olds and Buick were already in production. He was a businessman, and proved it when he was called in to sort out the ailing Henry Ford Company (Henry had

Second stage American: a 1921 Oldsmobile. With the buggy that he developed into the Curved Dash, Ransom Eli Olds was one of the founders of the US automotive industry

Gas station scene at Daytona in the mid-1920s. The first anti-knock tetraethyl gasoline was sold here in 1923

Remembered with affection—a Mercer Raceabout of 1922 at a rally in the USA

Over page *Modern Americans:* **top** *a 1972 Dodge Monaco.* **Middle** *a Chrysler Imperial Le Baron* and **bottom** *a 1972 Plymouth Fury Gran Sedan*

left to start the Ford Motor Co) in 1902. He rescued it from bankruptcy, renamed it the Cadillac Automobile Company (after Antoine de la Mothe Cadillac, who had founded Detroit) and began to make quality 6½ hp vehicles. He set fantastically high standards for the workmanship, quality control of which was illustrated by an experiment that took place in Britain in 1908. Three imported Cadillacs were dismantled and the parts 'scrambled' under scrutineers. They were re-assembled—and taken out on a 500 mile trip. No faults were found.

The standard is maintained today. As part of General Motors the name Cadillac is still the most aristocratic title in the Corporation, and indeed in the entire US automotive industry.

But a high standard of workmanship was not the only key to survival. In fact it often firmly locked the door to commercial viability. Many early manufacturers built cars of great quality, cars that were most advanced for their time. But some misjudged the market demands, some made too well and pushed costs too high, some made their machines so complex that very few could comprehend the intricacies of propelling the thing. Companies like Reeves of Columbus, Indiana, for instance, made an eight-wheel tourer on the principle of saving tyre-wear. In 1908, James Booth built a two-wheeler with miniature stabilising wheels which were hauled up when the car had achieved enough speed to be gyro-balanced. Not surprisingly, neither caught the public imagination greatly.

So many names disappeared in the first twenty years of the century—Vandergraft, Sphinx (a brief life from 1914 to 1915), Saginaw (1916; production: probably one), McCullogh (a two-seater made from 1899 all the way to 1900), Dragon, Dodo, Brownie, Cucmobile, Red Jacket, Red Bug, Red Arrow, to name but a few out of the thousands that perished after being offered to the public with high enthusiasm and higher hopes.

Some, now gone, still live in our memories; legendaries like Pierce-Arrow, Duesenberg, Mercer, Stutz, names that are like a roll-call of a great industrial past, foundation of the vigorous present. Others, born generations ago, are still with us—like Buick, Rambler (from 1902 through Jeffery, Nash and American Motors Corporation), Oldsmobile, Chevrolet (1911), Ford (1903), Dodge (1914), Cadillac.

The automobile reaches maturity

Scene: USA. Time: 1920–1940. This was the growing-up period in two ways. First, the cars themselves changed from 'early' to 'modern'. Secondly, production in the USA rose from 1,905,560 in 1920 to 3,717,385 in 1940. And it was 1949 before this second figure was to be exceeded by a significant margin.

We are now past the days of the Mercer Raceabout and the Stutz Bearcat (although Stutz are doing exciting things still), and the Duesenberg is having a shattering effect at the top end of the American scale. The Cord makes a formidable impact, and the Miller Special—with the great driver Frank Lockhart at the wheel—does remarkable things at Indianapolis and elsewhere.

Some US Firsts
While the automobile started as a European animal, its impact in the USA resulted in typically energetic response. 'Whilst others invent, Americans improve,' said an eminent engineer of the time—and so it was with the automobile. The list of US firsts (only a few were predated in Europe) is almost inexhaustible. On the right are just a few of those 'firsts' tabulated by 'Motor Trend':

Some of the Cars
There is but one car, during this period on the American scene, with which to start—the Duesenberg SJ. This supercharged version of the Model J was one of the most extraordinary cars ever produced, and was to typify aspects of American life at the most affluent end of the scale.

The car was so extrovert that it is too easy to overlook the truly astonishing technical qualities. It cost about ten times the price of a normal, large American car—but this was boom time and there were plenty of buyers to whom money was of little account. Some of them were William Randolph Hearst, Gary Cooper (two), Clark Gable, Mae West, the much-married multi-millionaire Tommy Manville, Joe E. Brown . . .

The straight eight of the standard Model J had a capacity approaching seven litres (420 cubic inches) and in spite of a compression ratio of only 5·2 to 1, the power output was claimed to be 265 bhp. The SJ, however, boasted no less than 320 bhp! Acceleration claimed for the

Air conditioning
An optional extra by Packard in 1938

Automatic transmission
While a centrifugal clutch with two speeds appeared in 1904 (Sturtevant), auto transmissions as we know them today came with the Oldsmobile offered with Hydra-Matic late in 1938

Brakes
(hydraulically operated on all four wheels). Duesenberg pioneered them as a production item in 1920, after the Lockheed development of 1917. However, there were custom-built examples earlier

Chromium plating
First in USA was Oldsmobile in 1925. Nickel had been used previously

Defroster vents
Chrysler Corporation, 1936

Directional signals
Buick, as an optional extra, 1938

Heater
1926 saw the first hot water heaters, as opposed to hot air ducted from the exhaust manifold. Several production cars appeared with them at the same time

Octane ratings
An octane rating for petrol/gasoline was drawn up by Dr Graham Edgar in the late 'twenties

Rubber engine mountings
Nash, 1922

Safety glass
Stutz, 1925. This was wired glass, a true 'first'. Rickenbacker introduced laminated in 1926, a year ahead of Ford making it standard in the Model A. Toughened glass became standard equipment on Chevrolets (for all windows) in 1940

Sixteen-cylinder engine
The first American example was by Cadillac late in 1929 (165 bhp)

Synchromesh
Developed and introduced in 1928 by Cadillac on their three-speed transmission

Below *The Duesenberg J, the most dramatic American car of its era. Housing a 6·9 litre motor, it outshone everything before it. This is a 1929 J*

Middle *First seen in 1932, the Duesenberg SJ, a supercharged version of the J, developed an almost-incredible 320 bhp. Clark Gable is in the driving seat*

Roadster was from zero to 100 mph in 17 seconds, and the top speed of the Phaeton was 104 mph (hold it–this was in second gear) and 129 in top. A specially prepared record car averaged 135·47 mph for twenty-four hours, and 152·1245 for one hour. Even 160 mph was exceeded.

When the Model J was unveiled at the New York Salon in 1928, it was said: 'for people of long established culture and wealth, possessing the inevitable good taste which accompanies these two characteristics, and the inclination to cater to it'. As no car had ever been built in the USA to compare with this powerful monster it was for years to be thought of by many as foreign. Writers in the 'thirties–partly because of its name–would often refer to it as German.

Only about three chassis (with right-hand drive) are known to have been sold in Great Britain, but they provided an interesting price comparison. A Rolls-Royce Phantom II chassis cost £1900, the Duesenberg J cost £2380.

Fred Duesenberg was killed in a car accident in 1932. An obituary in the *Motor* (USA) commented: 'Besides his pioneering of the supercharger for automobiles, four-wheel brakes, and his straight-eight engines, Duesenberg's use of many new engineering ideas was noteworthy throughout his life. He was the first to use hydraulically controlled four-wheel brakes, heat-treated molybdenum-steel frames, and balloon tyres on standard-production cars'.

Perhaps it is not surprising that another of the most interesting cars of the period, the Cord, came out under the same aegis. The original Duesenberg company had gone to the wall before the advent of the Models J and SJ, and in 1926 had been bought by Eric Lobban Cord, president of the Auburn Automobile Company. Cord had kept Fred Duesenberg to design and develop his 'masterpiece,' but the Cord in its own right was also of exceptional interest.

E. L. Cord was a remarkable man, building, like Fred Duesenberg, cars of exceptional quality and design. When the front-wheel-drive Cord appeared in 1929, the American *Motor* said: 'The Cord is obviously distinguished by the fact that it is the first really new automobile design to appear on the market for many years'. However, it was in 1936 that the Cord 810 made body-design history. It had headlamps that disappeared into the front wings and a wrap-round grille. But by this time innovations came too late, and the company folded within twelve months.

No record of American activity can leave out Stutz. Such readers as may go bug-eyed over the old 1914 Bearcat must remember that in 1928 a Stutz Black Hawk – a straight-eight with overhead camshaft – took second place in the 24-hour race at Le Mans, beating the record for the 5-litre category. In the previous year they were entered for all but one of the races organised by the AAA. They won every one.

In the story of American automobilism, Frank Lockhart's name seems to recur with one good reason after another. Now in connection with the Miller Special. The 1500 cc Miller engine was a famed piece of work, with twin overhead camshafts and a centrifugal supercharger. It could deliver 154 bhp at 7000 rpm, and in Lockhart's hands once reached 171·02 mph. Sadly, this great driver was later killed trying to beat the world's land speed record.

In 1933, there appeared a really good-looking Pierce (Silver) Arrow. In both appearance and performance it was years ahead of its time. The twelve-cylinder engine produced 175 bhp, and there was a free-wheel and power assisted brakes. The high standard of engineering and the finish were exceptional, but the production cost was too high to keep it going.

Manufacturer Eric L. Cord bought Duesenberg in 1926, but the Cord in its own right was of startling interest – particularly the 1936 model 810,

with its modern treatment. Headlamps vanished into wings and a wrap-round grille was used

Below *1920 to 1940 – the period in which the motor car grew up. This 1926 Chrysler 60 had smart lines and sophisticated engineering for its time*

Middle *Designed by driver Frank Lockhart, this boat-tailed Stutz 8 Speedster of 1928 was good for over 105 mph*

Meanwhile . . . back in Europe

The motoring scene in Europe was directly comparable in many ways. There was the similar variety of different makes and although very many lasted out until World War 2, most were to go to the wall in the great re-grouping of the 'fifties. One had established makes like Armstrong-Siddeley, Lea-Francis, Wolseley, Riley and so on in England; on the Continent the pattern of great variety was much the same. Sad it is, indeed, that so few of the names remain, and

that today so many are simply part of the amalgam of industrial facelessness.

However, during the 1920-1940 period, there were some great cars, still rightly treasured today. We can look at but a few here, in words or pictures. Painted on the British canvas was the 30/98 Vauxhall, derived from the earlier Prince Henry. This was the 'Car Superexcellent,' but it succumbed in 1927 when Vauxhall became simply a division of General Motors.

Then there were the classic Bentleys. W. O.

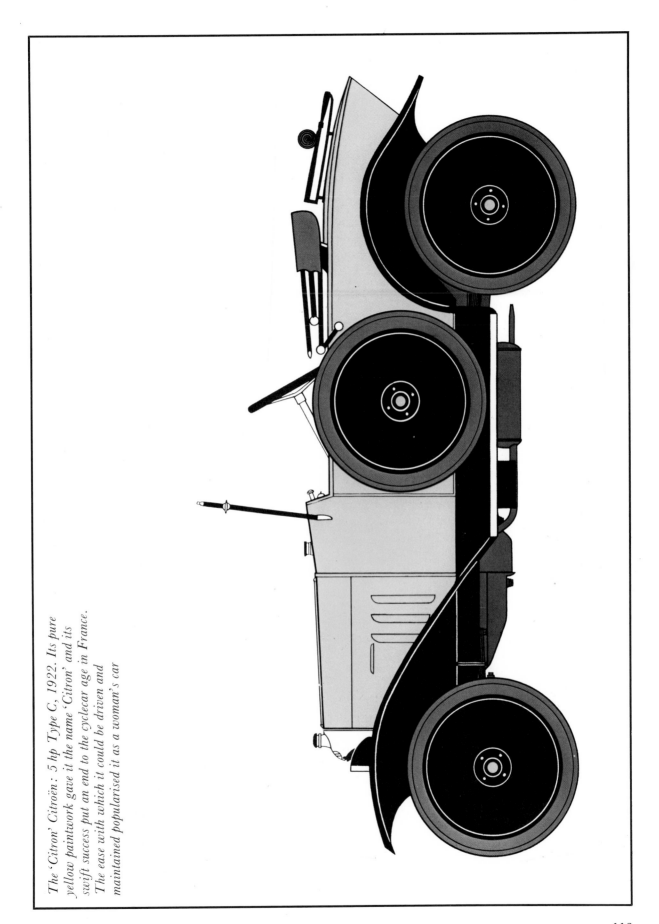

The 'Citron' Citroën: 5 hp Type C, 1922. Its pure yellow paintwork gave it the name 'Citron' and its swift success put an end to the cyclecar age in France. The ease with which it could be driven and maintained popularised it as a woman's car

Bentley's three-litre appeared in 1919 (and was tested for *The Autocar* by S. C. H. 'Sammy' Davis in that year) but it was not until late in 1921 that production got going. Bentleys had their heyday in the late 'twenties, Davis himself being one of the winners of the Twenty-four Hour race at Le Mans.

Mention must be made, too, of the 'chain gang' Frazer-Nash. A famous example was the 1930-37 TT Replica, with its front axle canti-

levered out on semi-elliptic springs well forward of the radiator. At the rear, the space was taken up by chains and dog clutches for the drive. A car with classic lines, and fun to drive.

While the side valve engine continued virtually without challenge in the USA, in Europe the pattern was different. Several makes not only had overhead valves, but one–or two–overhead camshafts. For example, in England even the little Morris Minor had an overhead camshaft driven (unusual, this) by the shaft of a vertically mounted generator. True, there was some trouble with oil dripping into the generator, but nevertheless this quite tiny (847 cc) engine was the basis of the famous MG Midget. The earliest version in 1929 developed only 20 bhp, but a later type with supercharger raised the power to 60 bhp!

As in the USA, the rich of Europe were rich indeed! And there were enough people with real wealth to produce an attractive market. Some makes are still with us to speak for themselves, like Rolls-Royce and Mercedes-Benz, but the rich were also catered for by Minerva (Belgium), Hispano-Suiza, Isotta-Fraschini, Renault, Leyland .

Top *A typical petrol station of the period, with an Armstrong Siddeley*

Above *Renault's first straight 8, the Reinastella Torpedo, had a 7·1 litre engine and, for the first time, a radiator at the front*

The Leyland was designed by Parry-Thomas of speed record fame and was the sensation of the 1920 motor show at Olympia: 'The most perfect car it is possible to design and manufacture'. On the other hand there was the 45 hp Renault for those who liked to buy their cars by the yard; this was the largest car to be built in any quantities in the 'twenties. The flavour of the Spanish Hispano designed by a Swiss (Suiza) and of the Italian Isotta were clearly defined by the novels of the day: the hero always drove an Hispano-Suiza and the villain an Isotta-Fraschini.

There was some reason for this romantic convention: the Hispano 6·6 litre overhead camshaft, 135 bhp engine was in a car that handled much better than the Isotta-Fraschini, so the hero always won in the chase. In this period Daimler (British variety) tried to dispel their funereal image with a 7·1 litre V-12 with double sleeve valves of frightening complexity.

The choice was wide, many of the engines complex and 'doubtful'. As one make remains pre-eminent today, it is perhaps because most people, in those days, played safe and bought a Rolls-Royce.

Below *Bentley 3 litre, 1922. Bentleys made their first appearance in 1919, went into full production in 1921*
Bottom *The Hispano-Suiza, a symbol of romance for many novelists. This is the 1924 product*

The latest British product from Ford is the Granada **above,** delivered in 2½ or 3 litre form, and designed for the executive, and from the United States in 1972, **below** this highly-styled Ford coupé

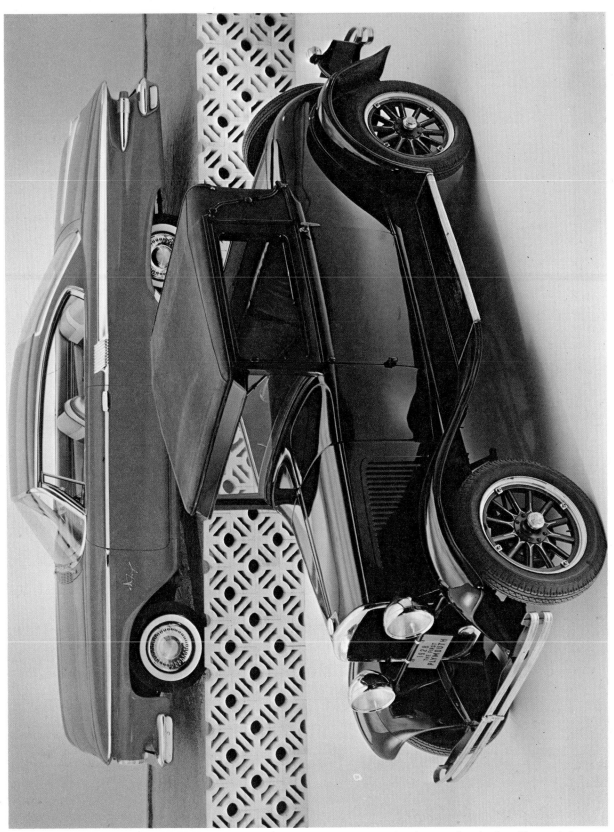

'An absolutely new development in the motor car style . . . slender chromium plated radiator, long low bodies . . . generous room for 2 to 5 passengers . . . beautiful bowl-type headlamps . . .'

So ran the advertisement for the first Plymouth in 1928. Here a 1928 model is exhibited with a 1961 Plymouth Fury

117

New technology of the 'fifties

First shown at the 1948 London Motor Show, the Jaguar XK120 was the sensation of the year. Here is *one lapping Silverstone in 1949, with Leslie Johnson conducting*

World War 2 put an end to commercial car construction; technological development in engineering was supercharged by the needs of war. At the war's end, motor manufacturers had to make use of their mothballed pre-war tooling. Not until around 1950 did production catch up with technology, and a completely new crop of cars flowered in public.

Probably the most significant developments were in body construction, engines and brakes. In Europe, excitement knew no bounds over the introduction of the Jaguar XK120 . . . then came the 'impossible' idea of putting such a power unit in a large family saloon! In the USA huge V-8s appeared, and the T-bird arrived on the scene. Back in Europe, Mercedes-Benz produced their memorable 300SL, and returned to motor racing with extraordinary success. This, we should remember, was the heyday of drivers like Juan Manuel Fangio and Stirling Moss.

In France, Citroën did the impossible by dropping models which they seemed to have been producing since before most of us had been born, and brought in the DS one of the most advanced vehicles of the day.

Engines – OHC

In considering engines, justice is served by taking a look at the XK120 unit. Not only was it the first major excitement in this area, but its continued success proved its worth. If it had two outstanding features they were the valvery and the appearance. (The purist will claim that the engine belonged to the late 1940s, but it was in the 1950s that it truly emerged, and indeed the first 'Autocar' road test report appeared in 1951). This period was the beginning of the end for the side valve engine. Jaguar scored so heavily by producing, at this early date, at a 'production price,' a *twin* overhead camshaft engine. And one of the design parameters was that it should look good. So the two camshaft covers on either side of the six in-line sparking plugs were beautifully polished – even to their neat rows of domed retaining nuts. When first exhibited, everyone assumed that the gleaming engine had been prepared as an exhibition job by an army of apprentices. But all the production units were also like that!

The early version developed some 160 bhp (at 5100 rpm). During the years, power output shot up, but at the time 160 was really something astonishing from 3·4 litres capacity. So was the top speed (for a not very costly production car) of 115 mph *within the distance available* as the 'Autocar' put it.

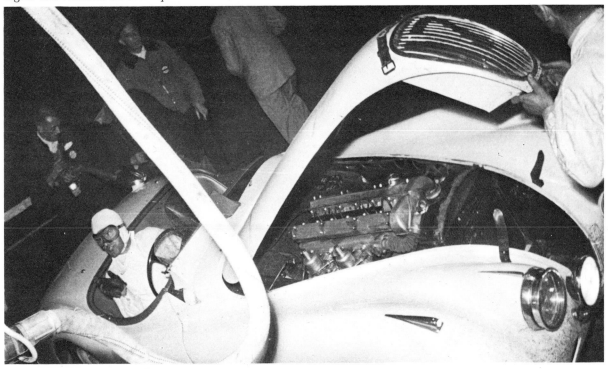

*XK120 at Le Mans during a pit-stop, showing the
engine that rendered all other sports cars obsolete*

Coachwork Advances

Bodywork is normally subject only to styling
changes, although more recently, crash safety
factors are a talking point. But the early 'fifties
saw the first major change in coachwork construction principle since the invention of
weatherproof designs. Previously, every car had
a chassis frame which acted as an anchor for the
body. But this period saw the emergence of 'unit
construction'. Of course, this is now standard
practice for mass-produced cars, but then it was
a breakthrough. In the event of crash damage,
the unit construction car could be more difficult
to repair, but at the same time, sadly, it was
realised that cars were not meant to last too long.
The term 'built-in obsolescence' arrived.

... and Transmissions

Transmissions were revolutionised by the advent
of the automatic gearbox. General Motors produced torque converters giving a variable ratio
on any one 'cog'. Hydramatic provided an
orthodox gearbox (in effect) which changed
automatically. For European drivers, who
needed precise control, the latter system was the
most favoured. But as the new transmissions
absorbed power they were not suitable at the
time for the average European car with its
comparatively small engine. A number of
European automatic transmissions, such as
Smiths' electro-pneumatic, made an appearance
to tempt the motor manufacturers in Europe –
but never really caught on. The exception was
provided when Holland re-entered car production with the DAF (Van Doorne's Automobiel-
fabrieken). This little car was fitted with notched
driving belts giving a variable, stepless transmission which, even today, continues to suit the
car well. However, this may have solved the
problem for very small, light cars, but not for
the average-sized European vehicle. Transmission problems were not entirely solved in the
'fifties – and have not been solved in the 'seventies
– but the start had been made.

Suspensions, Wheels and Tyres ...

Suspensions had their share of evolution.
Certainly Lancia had introduced a novel form
of independent front suspension on the legendary
Lambda in 1921-22, and IFS had appeared more
generally in the 'forties. However, it was in the
'fifties that IFS became standard practice and all-
round 'independence' almost common. This
period also saw the introduction of smaller road
wheels, which had their advantages but which,
to many, were a retrograde step, even allowing
for the smoother ride made possible by the new
suspensions.

Talk of wheels leads on to tyres, and in this area the 'fifties saw the biggest advance since John Boyd Dunlop made the pneumatic tyre a reality. Credit therefore to Michelin for the radial ply tyre. How this tyre's pros and cons were argued at the time! With steel bracing the ride was too hard at low speeds, said some. Faster drivers were overjoyed at the markedly improved road-holding, others equally pleased at the major increase in tyre mileage. But fast driving pessimists had dark thoughts—in the event of a skid, they said, the tyre breaks away without warning. In practice, it gave to most motorists a much larger safety margin, and more mileage.

Enter Discs

Disc brakes—again a development of the 'fifties with the honours going to Dunlop, and also to Jaguar for proving the product so dramatically. Theory and practice are now well known: instead of drums which can overheat, discs are mainly in the airstream with but a segment of pads held by high pressure against them. Thus came the non-fade brake. For Jaguar, it meant decisive wins in the 24-hour race at Le Mans, and for the public it meant a demand which enabled cost to fall to acceptable levels. Discs also allowed 'inboard' rear brakes, that is, beside the differential housing rather than in the hubs. Among sereral advantages was the reduction in unsprung weight.

Amongst the outstanding cars of this decade the Jaguar XK120 has been mentioned, but some reference should be made to the XK150, which is now in such demand for restoration. The Blue Top version of the engine was now giving 210 bhp and disc brakes were available.

Also there was more room. The mean maximum speed with overdrive had gone up to nearly 125 mph and the disc brakes showed an efficiency of 94 per cent g. Today, more than a decade later, there are few production cars in Britain at anywhere near the price—even allowing for inflation—that can seriously be considered as challengers.

The Mercedes 300SL first caught the eye in the 'fifties because of its gull-wing doors. It was always as well to lock them from the inside—to avoid taking off (if two flew up) or, (if one door came open) doing a victory roll! Here one had independent suspension all round, on a car that held the road like glue. Top speed from the 3 litre, six cylinder, 240 bhp engine gave a mean of 128·5 mph. On the debit side, it still had 'old fashioned' drum brakes with a maximum efficiency of around 87 per cent, but this was enough. The only problem was the price.

At the Paris Show in 1954 came US Ford's answer to European sports cars, the Thunderbird, modestly described by its manufacturers as a 'fast touring car'. This used a 5·1 litre V8 giving an unhurried 225 bhp, which in road terms meant a mean maximum speed of 113 mph. Brakes were still drums all round with an efficiency of 75 per cent. However, at this stage it must be confessed that the brakes on American cars were—for a variety of reasons—well below European standards.

No story of the 'fifties can finish without reference to the Citroën DS. The DS19 was—and is—particularly notable for the hydraulic system which actuated the suspension, brakes, automatic clutch, gear change and steering. And the suspension could be raised or lowered to suit road and driving conditions.

The XK120 was the first quantity-produced car to have a twin overhead camshaft engine

Enter discs—and the non-fade brake. The 1950s also saw all-round independent suspension in wider use

Below *The Mercedes 'Gull Wing' 300SL of the 1950s. This had a 3 litre 6-cylinder powerpack that gave a mean top speed of 128 mph*

Bottom *Citroën's contribution to technological advance was the DS19, introduced in 1955, with self-levelling suspension, power-assisted brakes, steering and gearchange. The body design was far ahead of the decade, and it took a year or two for its forward-looking philosophy to be accepted*

Classics of the future?

With London art auctioneers like Christie's and Sotheby's conducting old car sales on both sides of the Atlantic, fine automobiles have now acquired almost the same status as works of fine art from the past. And many of the cars that have been mentioned in earlier parts of this book are now sought after and highly prized.

Really ancient vehicles like a turn-of-the-century Benz sell for historic reasons; they are museum pieces, albeit still mobile ones. Cars of the 'thirties, like a supercharged $4\frac{1}{2}$ litre Bentley or a Bugatti Atlantique, are sought because they recall the days of hand-worked craftsmanship – and they have appreciated in value as much as 25 times in the last 25 years.

But more recent cars with claims to distinction are also fetching higher prices today than they did when they were new. Among them are the Jaguar XK range and the AC Ace of the 'fifties, the Lotus Elite which spanned the 'fifties and 'sixties and the Daimler SP250 of the early 'sixties.

What decides which cars become worthy of collecting? One dealer has said, a trifle cynically, 'The cars to back are those whose makers have gone out of business,' and this certainly applies to makes like the Gordon-Keeble and the Healey.

But it is by no means the complete answer. And although prices may be highest for cars which were produced in small numbers – and so have a rarity-value – certain mass-produced popular motors are also in demand. For instance, some 15 million Model T Fords were built, yet they can now reach 10 times their original price.

So the question poses itself: which of the cars of the nineteen-seventies will be the classics of the twenty-first century?

Recent years have brought cars of revolutionary and advanced design like the NSU Ro 80, the first to make use of the rotary Wankel engine. But the car was attended by so many birth pangs it can hardly be regarded as an instant success.

The 'seventies have also brought many sound, conventional uninspired bread-and-butter cars like the Morris Marina (known in the United States as the Austin Marina). But it is difficult to imagine the Marina as a collector's item of the future.

Are these, then, the cars of the 'seventies that may become classics . . .?

Citroën of France. Always in the forefront in new design principle, this company has a contender for the

Classics of the Future in the little 1015 cc GS

From Germany, the source of some of the finest cars of recent years. In the view of many, Mercedes are making the greatest cars in the world, and two models already stand out as possible classics. They are the mighty Mercedes 300 SEL with its 6·3 litre automatic V8 engine which blends high performance (135 mph) with great comfort and dignity behind its traditional Mercedes radiator and conservative appearance; and the 350 SL, successor to the time-honoured 280 SL. This two-seater has a 3½ litre V8 engine (4½ litre in the USA) and has become something of a heavyweight in its inclusion of safety features to satisfy American requirements.

And the Porsche 911 has developed a long way from the original Beetle concept in its emergence as a rear-engine GT car capable of 140 mph from its 2342 cc engine, one of three engine options in the range.

From France. Citroën produced their finest engineering achievement with the SM, powered by a special Maserati V6 engine of 2670 cc giving 170 bhp at 5500 rpm and a speed of 135 mph. It still has the traditional Citroën nose and has the usual Citroën all-independent hydro-pneumatic self-levelling suspension and pressurised brakes, plus a novel power-centring system.

And at the other end of the spectrum Citroën produced a most advanced little car in the 1015 cc 90 mph GS, which was hailed as a Car of the Year in 1970, long before most critics had had the opportunity to drive one.

From Britain. Jaguar have long enjoyed the reputation of giving value for money and seldom have they given more than with the Jaguar XJ6, a saloon embodying 'grace and pace' and admired by the cognoscenti from its inception in 1968. The 4·2 litre engine gives it a top speed of 120 mph with a superb ride – a certain future classic, this one.

A V12 power unit is employed in the Jaguar E Type and has given the third series of this sports model a new character. Over the ten years of its life, the E-type has become wider and heavier but the new 5·3 litre engine with its four

continued on page 126

Dignity with power; the Mercedes 300 SEL

For Classics one must return to the finest in German engineering, the Porsche. Here is the 2 litre 6-cylinder 911S

Motor sport now: 2

Top *US pilot Peter Revson takes the F1 Yardley McLaren Ford M19A round the circuit at speed. Grand Prix racing costs have soared in recent years— the 2993 cc 8-cylinder Ford engine alone costs £6500*

Above *Brazil's World Champion Emerson Fittipaldi chats to a tobacco company 'hostess' on the grid just before the start of a Formula 1 race*
Opposite page *The noisy end*

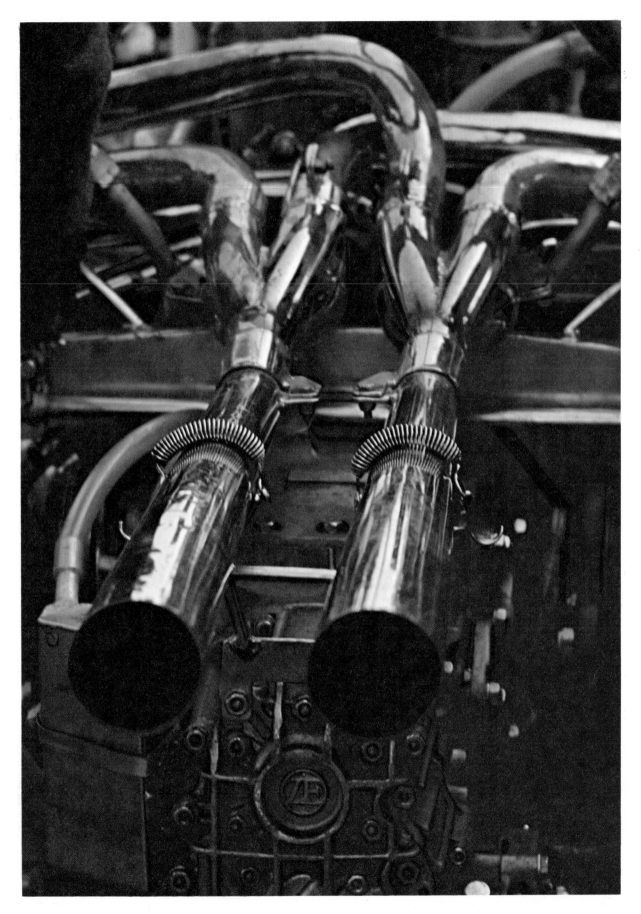

continued from page 123

Zenith carburettors have given it a zesty 145 mph performance.

Another British high-performance luxury car is the Jensen Interceptor III, though in fact it is Italian designed and American powered. It uses a 6·3 litre Chrysler V8 engine with standard automatic transmission, and is superbly quiet and beautifully equipped even to stereo radio, and courtesy lights that remain on for 30 seconds after the doors are shut!

For a really unconventional possible classic, consider the go-anywhere, do almost anything Range Rover.

From Italy. The names that come to mind immediately are those makers of superb high-performance thoroughbred machinery, Lamborghini and Ferrari. Lamborghini produce the Miura SV of four litres and Ferrari the 365 GTB4 Daytona of 4·3 litres. But both have V12 engines and both are motorway expresses with a performance of around 173 mph.

Yet Italy has also produced one of the greatest small cars of recent years in the Fiat 128, winner

Interior of the Jensen Interceptor III from Britain, although Italian-designed and powered by an American unit

Britain: the V12 power unit employed by the Jaguar E-Type has given the third series of this model a new character

One of the greatest small cars of recent years – the Fiat 128, winner of several Car-of-the-Year awards in 1970

of half-a-dozen Car of the Year awards in 1970. The engine is only 1116 cc and the top speed is a mere 87 mph, yet it can run rings around most cars in its class at the traffic lights. And although it is only 12 feet 8 inches long, the designers have managed to devote 80 per cent of the space to the passengers, giving them more leg-room than many bigger vehicles.

From the USA. Most American cars of recent years have been unexciting, but one exception is the Chevrolet Camaro 350SS. It embodies lessons learned from Europe, and uses a 5·7 litre V8 engine in a sleek, fine riding, wide-wheeled body only 15 feet 8 inches long.

From Japan. Although still regarded with some suspicion in European countries, the Japanese motor industry has made incredible strides in auto-engineering in recent years, and the flag car has been the rally-winning Datsun 240Z, a two-seater GT coupé with a six-cylinder 2·4 litre engine giving a top speed of 125 mph.

These then are some of the cars that could be among the classics of tomorrow. One is tempted to hedge the bet . . . to include products of Alfa-Romeo, Toyota, VW and Ford. But the list would grow too long. The flops can be written off quickly and easily; the cars with character which will outlive the decade take longer to assess.

The Chevrolet Camaro embodies lessons learned from Europe, with more than a touch of American power in its pack

From Japan, the Datsun 240Z, 1972

Modern Italian, the ultimate in motoring maturity!
A Ferrari Dino, 1972